AIR FORCE FELLOWS

COLLEGE OF AEROSPACE DOCTRINE, RESEARCH AND EDUCATION

AIR UNIVERSITY

The Influence of Politics, Technology, and Asia on the Future of US Missile Defense

Lieutenant Colonel, USAF

Walker Paper No. 7

Air University Press
Maxwell Air Force Base, Alabama 36112-5962

August 2007

Muir S. Fairchild Research Information Center Cataloging Data

Butler, Jeffrey T.
   The influence of politics, technology, and Asia on the future of US missile defense / Jeffrey T. Butler.
      p. ; cm. – (Walker paper, 1555-7871 ; no. 7)
      Includes bibliographical references.

   1. Ballistic missile defenses—United States. 2. United States—Foreign relations—Asia. 3. Asia—Foreign relations—United States. I. Title. II. Series.

   358.1/74/0973—dc22

Disclaimer

Opinions, conclusions, and recommendations expressed or implied within are solely those of the author and do not necessarily represent the views of Air University, the United States Air Force, the Department of Defense, or any other US government agency. Cleared for public release: distribution unlimited.

This Walker Paper and others in the series are available electronically at the Air University Research Web site http://research.maxwell.af.mil and the AU Press Web site http://aupress.maxwell.af.mil.

Air Force Fellows

Since 1958 the Air Force has assigned a small number of carefully chosen, experienced officers to serve one-year tours at distinguished civilian institutions studying national security policy and strategy. Beginning with the 1994 academic year, these programs were accorded in-residence credit as part of professional military education at senior service schools. In 2003 these fellowships assumed senior developmental education (SDE) force-development credit for eligible officers.

The SDE-level Air Force Fellows serve as visiting military ambassadors to their centers, devoting effort to expanding their colleagues' understanding of defense matters. As such, candidates for SDE-level fellowships have a broad knowledge of key Department of Defense (DOD) and Air Force issues. SDE-level fellows perform outreach by their presence and voice in sponsoring institutions. They are expected to provide advice as well as promote and explain Air Force and DOD policies, programs, and military-doctrine strategy to nationally recognized scholars, foreign dignitaries, and leading policy analysts. The Air Force Fellows also gain valuable perspectives from the exchange of ideas with these civilian leaders. SDE-level fellows are expected to apprise appropriate Air Force agencies of significant developments and emerging views on defense as well as economic and foreign policy issues within their centers. Each fellow is expected to use the unique access she or he has as grounds for research and writing on important national security issues. The SDE Air Force Fellows include the National Defense Fellows, the RAND Fellows, the National Security Fellows, and the Secretary of Defense Corporate Fellows. In addition, the Air Force Fellows program supports a post-SDE military fellow at the Council on Foreign Relations.

On the level of intermediate developmental education, the chief of staff approved several Air Force Fellowships focused on career broadening for Air Force majors. The Air Force Legislative Fellows program was established in April 1995, with the Foreign Policy Fellowship and Defense Advanced Research Projects Agency Fellowship coming under the Air Force Fellows program in 2003. In 2004 the Air Force Fellows also assumed responsibility for the National Laboratories Technologies Fellows.

Contents

Tables

Photographs

Foreword

In recent years the phrase "since the end of the Cold War" has constituted the prologue for scenarios based on the assumption that we have entered a somehow less dangerous phase of world affairs. That is far from self-evident. To mention that but two elements bring this supposition into question:

1. Proliferation has confronted us with regimes compared with which the late Soviet Union appeared "rational," or at least predictable, certainly if viewed within its own context. Consequently, even a highly questionable supposition like "mutually assured destruction" could act as a stabilizer, at least for a short period. Now, however, one has to deal with international actors (rogue states and their terrorist clients) that must be regarded as "irrational" by any standards of international behavior.

2. Russia itself, while certainly no longer an ideological opponent, has embarked upon a neo-imperial path (initially against the other former Soviet republics) that has been shrugged off by many because of the visible decline of Russia's military capability. What has been overlooked is the fact that this very weakness in "conventional" weapons has driven Russia to place far greater emphasis on nuclear intercontinental ballistic missiles. In that sense, a putative confrontation seems more likely to precipitate resort to weapons of mass destruction (WMD).

In the light of these developments, missile defense has become a key factor in US strategic planning. The problem, of course, lies with the stage of current technological development. Mid-course or terminal-phase systems appear closer to feasibility just now, at least theoretically. Unfortunately, these constitute the least satisfactory answers to missile attacks.

Much further away from realization is a (putative) space-based system aimed at destroying hostile missile launchings during the boost phase. That, however, seems to be the one way missile defense can come close to eliminating the threat without huge collateral damage (that would result from a terminal-phase system). Unfortunately it provides only a very brief time span for making the decision that a launch is taking place and acting accordingly. Failing an effective boost-phase system, the only effective answer would lie in preemptive action, with all of its international ramifications.

It is one of the many virtues of Col Jeffrey Butler's deeply reflective and expert analysis of this complex and highly troubling issue that he does not avoid confronting all of the problematic and, at this stage theoretical, solutions to what may be deemed the number one security threat facing the United States. He approaches the political issues no less deftly than the complex technical questions. Despite the need for the latter, the result is a fluent and highly readable product. This is a very important work, and one hopes that it will receive the attention it deserves. The US Air Force is to be congratulated, not merely for producing such outstanding officers, but for having had the vision to create a symbiotic relationship with the, alas relatively few, academic institutions that have not only welcomed this association but have known how to make the most of the academic-military relationship.

The Institute for the Study of Conflict Ideology and Policy (ISCIP) has been a particularly fortunate beneficiary of the Air Force's National Defense Fellows program. Under it, these officers have been integrated fully into ISCIP's in-depth, analytical research program, which addresses the problems posed by developments in the post-Soviet arena. The result has enhanced immeasureably the military insights reflected in the program's publications, while providing the Air Force officers with unusual information concerning the political context.

Colonel Butler's work, as has been the case with some of his predecessors in the program, constitutes the culmination of a mutually beneficial relationship, and we are deeply appreciative to have been given the opportunity to be associated with this publication.

Uri Ra'anan
Director, Institute for the Study
of Conflict Ideology and Policy
Boston, Massachusetts

About the Author

Lt Col Jeffrey T. Butler

Lt Col Jeffrey T. Butler, USAF, is a National Defense Fellow at Boston University, Massachusetts, performing research on Russia, Central Asia, and international military affairs. His experience spans a wide variety of acquisition, technology, space, and intelligence assignments. Colonel Butler holds an undergraduate degree in mathematics from the US Air Force Academy, graduate degrees in military studies and electrical engineering, and a doctorate in computer engineering from the Air Force Institute of Technology. He is also a graduate of Air Command and Staff College and Air War College.

Abstract

This paper discusses the United States' need for a limited missile-defense system and the political, technical, and diplomatic forces which define the requirements. The end of the Cold War, weapons of mass destruction proliferation, and rise of terrorism challenge the utility of mutually assured destruction. This new context demands renewed consideration of strategic defense with emphasis on the true technical maturity and political costs. Like nuclear weapons, ballistic missile defenses have high political and psychological value that must be evaluated as intensely as the technology. Thus, the US engagement strategy toward Asia must also be informed by an understanding of security relationships, technology, and the unique role of domestic US politics.

In the near term, the United States should only pursue a limited ballistic missile-defense system with emphasis on theater systems and countering long-range missiles from the handful of rogue states that are pursuing them. Concurrently, the United States must improve threat definition, demand increased technical maturity and testing, and pursue flexible systems that can perform militarily significant missions in addition to missile defense. Furthermore, engagement with friends and foes is essential to developing an effective missile-defense system, maximizing deterrence value and supporting other critical efforts such as WMD counterproliferation and intelligence gathering. This strategy will reduce the technical risk of missile defense, increase the United States' freedom of action against a rising cadre of WMD-capable actors, and avoid unnecessary escalation in tension between the United States and Asia.

Preface

As the son of a United States Army infantryman growing up in Cold War Germany, I was fascinated and encouraged by Pres. Ronald Reagan's vision to create a missile-defense shield that would end the threat of nuclear-tipped missiles. The post–Cold War world is in many ways more chaotic than it was 20 years ago. Furthermore, the ballistic missile threat is also more chaotic, which has reinvigorated a personal desire to once again investigate the usefulness and feasibility of missile defense. For the purposes of this study, "Russian" and "Russia" will be used to refer to the successor state of the Soviet Union.

The US government has a moral obligation to defend its people, and the idea of intentionally remaining vulnerable to attack is unsettling. Yet technology has limits, and it is not possible to eliminate or defend against all threats. As the old cliché goes, "those who attempt to defend against everything will defend against nothing." Critics argue President Reagan's dream is unachievable due to the limits of technology and diplomacy. However, there is a definite role and need for a more limited missile-defense vision if it is bounded by realistic and accurate assessments of threats, technology, and the international environment.

I extend my sincere appreciation for everyone who assisted in the preparation of this paper. I am thankful for the support and camaraderie of Boston University's Institute for the Study of Conflict Ideology and Policy with special thanks to Prof. Uri Ra'anan, soon to be Dr. Susan Cavan, Lt Col John Kafer, and LCDR Marcel Leblanc. I also owe a tremendous debt of gratitude to Massachusetts Institute of Technology (MIT)/Lincoln Lab engineers and program managers who provided outstanding insight and background on missile-defense technology. One of my best experiences as an Air Force Fellow was participating in seminars with Professors Theodore Postol (MIT), Rob Pfaltzgraff (Tufts/Fletcher School), Neta Crawford (Boston University), and Don Babai (Harvard). Their knowledge, experience, and enthusiasm were superb.

Finally, I give my highest thanks to God who placed me at Covenant Church. This was a great blessing for me as well as my wife, Dawn, and daughters, Sarah and Gracie, all of whom I love very much.

Chapter 1

Introduction

What if free people could live secure in the knowledge that their security did not rest upon the threat of instant U.S. retaliation to deter a Soviet attack, that we could intercept and destroy strategic ballistic missiles before they reached our own soil or that of our allies?

I know this is a formidable, technical task, one that may not be accomplished before the end of the century. Yet, current technology has attained a level of sophistication where it's reasonable for us to begin this effort. It will take years, probably decades of efforts on many fronts. There will be failures and setbacks, just as there will be successes and breakthroughs.

—Pres. Ronald Reagan
23 March 1983

Since the World War II terror bombings of London by German V-1 and V-2 rockets, nations have desired a means to protect their homeland, populace, and fielded forces from missile attack. The addition of the weapons of mass destruction (WMD) to ballistic missiles further increases the motivation for defense. However, ballistic missile defense (BMD) is a difficult challenge, and the massive buildup of missiles in the Cold War reflected the dominance of strategic offense over the limited ability to defend.

The end of the Cold War reduced nuclear tension between the United States, Europe, and Russia; but conversely, the threat of ballistic-missile attack has increased. Several reasons for the increased threat include the rise of global terror, proliferation of missile technology and WMDs, the acceptance of the use of theater ballistic missiles in conventional combat, and the increasing number and belligerence of unstable states primarily in the Middle East and Asia. For example, the "war of the cities" between Iran and Iraq demonstrated the confluence between missile technology proliferation and an emerging willingness to use ballistic missiles in combat as opposed to merely a deterrent. Moreover, the single, most costly Iraqi attack against

US forces in Operation Desert Storm resulted from a Scud ballistic missile.[1]

The change in the nature of the ballistic-missile threat reinvigorated the flame initially sparked by President Reagan's "star wars" or Strategic Defense Initiative (SDI). Indeed, missile defense was signed into law by Pres. William J. "Bill" Clinton in 1999 and is one of the highest priorities of Pres. George W. Bush's administration. The terrorist attacks of 11 September 2001 (9/11) and the subsequent military interventions in Afghanistan and Iraq pushed the missile-defense issue off the front page. While the public debate is less vocal, much uncertainty still remains on which policy the United States should pursue on national missile defense and the resultant impact on global affairs. Among the chief issues are the true nature of the threat, the technical and operational feasibility of fielding missile defenses, and the impact on global stability.

The US strategy toward national missile defense should also be informed by an understanding of foreign defense priorities and perceptions. Understanding perceptions is important because much like nuclear weapons, BMDs have high political and psychological value which must be appreciated as intensely as technical capability. For example, the public debate on missile defense in the US tends to focus on intercontinental ballistic missiles (ICBM). However, many nations are more concerned about short- or medium-range theater ballistic missiles because their arch rivals are right next door. For example, a poorly planned introduction of theater missile defense in Taiwan will create a strong regional response from China which considers the issue of vital national interest. Consequently, US missile-defense policy must accurately appreciate the strategic impact of all forms of missile defense on other nations to include short- as well as long-range missile defense.

The political impact of US missile-defense policy is particularly important with respect to Asia as this continent will be the geopolitical focus of ballistic-missile and WMD concerns for the next decade. There are several critical actors with regard to missile defense in Asia. Russia has unique importance for US policy in the near term. Russia's overall military decline is well documented, but it continues to promote and improve its ballistic-missile force as the primary source of deterrence and military relevancy. Russia also recognizes its own vulnerability to Islamic extremism and WMD proliferation as illustrated by the bloody insurgency in Chechnya. Russia's unique combination of WMD know-how but strong incentive to maintain the status quo in the region makes it a potential partner in maintaining stability in Asia.

Beyond Russia, the emerging nuclear powers of Asia also impact US missile-defense policy. US plans may have the most impact on China which maintains a minimum nuclear-deterrent force of approximately 20 ICBMs capable of reaching the United States. China is already engaged in a massive military expansion campaign, and even a limited US missile-defense system could cause further escalation in the number of Chinese ballistic missiles. Similarly, India and Pakistan are drawn into the mix as multiple, competing alliances create uncertainties and possibly destabilize the region. The political utility of missile defense is readily apparent by its value in negotiations such as with North Korea and alliance building with nations such as Japan and Israel. Clearly, Asian diplomacy will influence the success or failure of US missile-defense plans.

Chapter 2 provides a background in the genesis of the current US missile-defense program that is essential to understanding the political, technical, and diplomatic forces which shaped the existing strategy. Chapter 3 assesses the systems in development and early stages of deployment with emphasis on system architecture, affordability, and technical realism. Asian reaction to the US missile-defense program is described in chapter 4 along with an analysis of the forces that drive Asian strategic defense policies. Recommendations and conclusions for the US missile-defense program are defined in chapter 5.

Note

(All notes appear in shortened form. For full details, see the appropriate entry in the bibliography.)

1. Donovan, *Terrorism Project.*

Chapter 2

Déjà vu All Over Again

The decision to build a defense to protect the United States from missile attack is a crucial political issue facing the Bush administration and Congress. This is the third time that missile defense has risen to the top of the national policy agenda.

—Senator John Warner
Senate Armed Services Committee

Failure is not a crime. Failure to learn from failure is.

—Walter Wriston

The United States has pursued BMD at varying levels of intensity since early in the Cold War as alluded to by Senator Warner's quote. Early incarnations of missile defense were focused against the Soviet Union; however, the prospects for adequately defending against a massive attack were slim resulting in the acceptance of the mutually assured destruction (MAD) doctrine. This conclusion was codified in the 1972 Anti-Ballistic Missile (ABM) Treaty which severely curtailed ABM deployments.

The ballistic missile debate reemerged in the 1980s with President Reagan's Strategic Defense Initiative. The technical and political realities of the 1990s reduced the SDI vision from an all-encompassing global defense to the more limited system now in development. A key milestone in the current debate was the dissolution of the 1972 ABM Treaty by the United States in 2002. Internationally, the ABM Treaty was considered a pillar of global nuclear stability. The end of the ABM Treaty, along with a concerted effort by the United States to field a layered defense, has intensified the international debate on the merits and dangers of missile defense. The following sections detail events from 1960 to the present in order to demonstrate the substantial influence of politics, technology limitations, and international relations on US missile-defense policy.

Missile Defense in the Cold War

The US and Soviet investigation into missile defense began after World War II. The unprecedented German V-1 and V-2 terror bombings of London were a chief culprit in initiating a desire to defend against ballistic-missile attack. Following the war, both nations rushed to acquire German missile technology to add to their own arsenals. This process uncovered German plans to build multistage long-range missiles potentially capable of ocean-spanning strikes around the world. While the emerging missile technology provided the potential for global range, the advent of nuclear weapons provided a compact payload capable of horrific destruction. Not surprisingly, the combination of ballistic missiles with WMDs initiated a serious investigation into strategic defense by both the Soviet Union and the United States.

Missile defense, as well as virtually the entire national-security enterprise, received heightened attention following the successful launch of the *Sputnik* satellite in 1957. Russia's ability to launch a satellite into orbit removed any doubt about the reality of the ICBM threat; and in 1958, the US Army accelerated development of the first US missile-defense system, the Nike-Zeus, that was successfully tested in 1962.

The Nike-Zeus system achieved several technical objectives, but it also revealed numerous issues that continue to plague missile-defense systems even today. First, the overall system was extremely complex and expensive. The system required four different types of radars that had to work in conjunction with

- detecting the incoming missile,

- discriminating the warhead from other objects,

- tracking the warhead,

- and then guiding the Nike-Zeus missile to the intercept point.

Beyond the complexity, radar technology of the era was ill-suited to performing target discrimination at the required ranges resulting in a high likelihood of tracking the rocket body as opposed to the warhead. The cost for the system was also unattractive as estimates for fielding even a limited system

6

were much greater than $15 billion for a system with questionable effectiveness.[1]

A second major issue was developing an effective kill vehicle. The quality of radar tracking was not adequate for a conventional warhead; therefore, the Nike-Zeus and all other ABM systems of this era used nuclear warheads to compensate for the lack of accuracy. Indeed, the Nike-Zeus and Spartan systems used megaton-plus warheads because the guidance systems were accurate only to a few kilometers. For reference, the atomic bombs dropped on Hiroshima and Nagasaki were less than 20 kilotons.

The use of nuclear warheads on the ABM interceptors created several issues. A prime concern was the potential for catastrophic collateral damage. The Starfish Prime experiment of 1962 demonstrated the devastating effects of detonating a nuclear weapon in space.[2] The radiation and ionization (electromagnetic pulse or EMP) created by the detonation would cause immediate physical damage to satellites in the line of site as well as disrupt ground radars and communication systems. Consequently, the first detonation would likely blind the missile-defense radars and the command-and-control system disrupting the ability to intercept subsequent missiles. An additional issue was the prospect of an ABM warhead falling on friendly soil due to a malfunction or unsuccessful intercept. These concerns in addition to other issues created tremendous controversy over the use of nuclear warheads in ABM missiles.

Finally, the rapidly increasing number, complexity, and geographic dispersal of ballistic missiles decreased the likelihood of fielding a credible missile defense in the 1960s. By the middle of the 1960s, the United States and Russia were firmly engaged in an ICBM arms race with rapidly expanding arsenals which could easily overwhelm any realistically conceivable defense. In addition, ICBMs were becoming more difficult to intercept with the development of multiple-warheads / single-missile combinations with the intentional inclusion of decoys and electronic countermeasures such as chaff to overwhelm the already weak target discrimination and tracking radars. Targeting complexity also increased as both the United States and Russia developed tactics for ingress (e.g. multiple approaches, leader/follower, and staged arrival) that would easily render the available missile defenses impotent while allowing the majority of missiles to reach their objectives.[3] Additionally, the locations of deployed missiles increased during the 1960s to include the arrival of the submarine-launched ballistic missile (SLBM). The need to constantly search for thousands of warheads coming from virtually any direction with effective decoys was too much for a realistic defense.

The policy and strategy debate continued strong in the United States, but the clear inadequacy of the available missile-defense technology along with Soviet willingness to discuss arms limitations led to the 1972 ABM Treaty. While there was little disagreement over the validity and nature of the threat, the US missile-defense debate in the 1960s was nonetheless intense and acrimonious. Advocates of missile defense acknowledged technical limitations but believed that even a defense of limited utility would save lives. Moreover, many advocates pointed to a moral issue with the doctrine of MAD which would put the United States at risk without even trying to defend itself. Conversely, opponents of missile defense pragmatically highlighted the clear inability to field an effective missile defense at any cost.

Ultimately, the belief in the overwhelming superiority of offensive strategic forces ended the pursuit of a comprehensive strategic defense. Defense Secretary Robert S. McNamara and many other influential defense strategists became increasingly skeptical of missile defense and embraced offensive deterrence through MAD.[4] Missile defense was considered potentially destabilizing because the United States and Russia might engage in an even greater arms race to overcome the opponents defense leading to larger numbers of weapons. Convinced of the futility of missile defense, McNamara advocated abandoning the effort; however, international and political factors conspired to keep the program alive in a more limited role.

Competition with Russia, increasing concern over China, and domestic politics led to Pres. Lyndon B. Johnson supporting a limited ABM system. In 1964 US intelligence discovered the development and deployment of the Soviet Galosh ABM system situated around Moscow.[5] President Johnson and McNamara lobbied the Russians to abstain from fielding the missile-defense system, but Russia disregarded the overture and continued unabated. As Soviet premier Alexey Kosygin stated,

"When I have trouble sleeping at night, it's because of your offensive missiles, not your defensive missiles."[6] Furthermore, China surprised the world by detonating its first nuclear weapon in 1960, launching a guided nuclear missile in 1966, and then demonstrating a hydrogen bomb in 1967.[7] Russia's intransigence combined with the emerging China threat reenergized the missile-defense debate.

Politically, President Johnson feared the perception of an "ABM gap" would hurt the Democrats in the 1968 elections and consequently tasked McNamara to find a compromise. McNamara strongly believed that a defense against Russia was not feasible. Instead, he proposed a limited system designed to counter the Chinese threat. This system would appease the ABM lobby by providing a US capability while not escalating the arms race with Russia. Hence, in 1967, the Sentinel program was born that sought to protect a limited number of population sites by fielding a "layered" defense against Chinese missiles. Much like the current missile-defense programs, "the Sentinel decision represented a political compromise—an attempt to balance conflicting strategic, technical, and diplomatic considerations."[8]

The Sentinel decision temporarily quelled the political debate, but it led to a more public debate on missile defense that once again impacted the nation's missile-defense plans. Academic and scientific groups such as the Federation of American Scientists (FAS) became increasingly vocal opponents of missile defense. Several leading academics, including members of influential presidential advisory panels, published articles describing the vulnerability of missile defenses. In addition, public opposition materialized in areas where the Army planned to locate missile-defense sites as local citizens feared their homes becoming attractive targets for Chinese or Russian missiles. Hence, by 1969, support for even a limited missile defense was losing ground prompting yet another shift in missile-defense policy.

Pres. Richard M. Nixon elected to make more changes to the missile-defense program early in his presidency which set the final course for its demise. As is often the custom with troubled programs, the program name was changed from Sentinel to Safeguard. In addition, Nixon changed the focus of the system from population defense to protecting strategic missiles from attack. This had the politically expedient advantage of moving the missiles away from population centers to more-remote areas. However, the change in focus undercut the already tenuous credibility of defending the US population against Chinese missile attack. Thus, by the end of 1969, no coherent imperative remained to field a missile defense, and the primary value of the Safeguard system was as a bargaining chip in the ongoing Strategic Arms Limitation Talks (SALT) as clearly detailed in declassified memos from the Nixon administration.[9]

The SALT discussions produced a watershed agreement between the United States and Russia to accept mutual vulnerability and virtually eliminate strategic defense. This agreement was codified in the 1972 ABM Treaty, which limited each nation to two land-based ABM sites with no more than 100 missiles at a site. A subsequent agreement in 1974 reduced the number of sites from two down to a single location. The acceptance of the ABM Treaty and other aspects of the SALT agreement dealt a crippling blow to US missile-defense plans. In 1975 the United States fielded a Safeguard site in North Dakota, but Congress cancelled funding for the program due to high costs, likely ineffectiveness, and fears over the use of nuclear-tipped interceptors. The Safeguard site was shut down in 1976, just five months after startup at a cost of over $5 billion (fiscal year [FY] 76) which is nearly $30 billion today.[10] Curiously, the secretary of defense presiding over the shutdown of the Safeguard system was Mr. Donald Rumsfeld, a man who would later become very instrumental in resurrecting the effort decades later.

Star Wars

The US missile-defense program and debate from the 1980s to the present has much in common with the previous phase from World War II to 1976. Although technology has advanced, the ability to hit a "bullet with a bullet" remains a difficult and financially costly challenge. Beyond technology, the role of domestic politics, international security, and fear of the unknown greatly affected missile-defense policy early in the Cold War and continue to play a foundational role in post–Cold War decision making. Similar to nuclear missiles or terrorism, discourse on long-range ballistic missile defense transcends purely technical discussions and evokes strong passion in both supporters and advocates. President Reagan tapped into these passions when he ignited the second era of national-missile-defense discussions with SDI.

President Reagan initiated the largest peacetime military buildup in US history upon his entry into office. His initial plan did not include missile defense, but supporters seized the opportunity to lobby for missile defense, given the increasing size of the Soviet nuclear arsenal and a nascent belief in emerging "hit-to-kill" technology. The Army continued with ABM research after the end of the Safeguard program by focusing on kinetic kill technology that would eliminate the need for a nuclear interceptor. Army test results in the late 1970s and early 1980s demonstrated improved interceptor accuracy. ABM advocates used these results as evidence of the ability to guide an ABM interceptor to destroy a ballistic missile through a direct physical impact without the need for a nuclear warhead.

In 1983 Reagan stunned the world by announcing the SDI to investigate the feasibility of providing a global shield against nuclear missiles. Reagan's grand vision was to render nuclear weapons unnecessary through development of a nonnuclear, impenetrable shield to shoot down ICBMs. While derisively called "Star Wars" by critics, much of the defense establishment jumped on the missile-defense bandwagon following Reagan's landslide reelection in 1984.[11] Thus, reminiscent of the push following the *Sputnik* launch, missile defense received new birth in the growing nationalism and idealism inspired by Reagan.

Remarkably, just as questions of technical maturity, cost, and politics battered missile-defense programs of the 1960s, these same issues changed the course of SDI. By 1986 the euphoria over SDI subsided. Moreover even supporters acknowledged costs to field a comprehensive missile shield would be hundreds of billions of dollars. Internationally, relations with Russia were improving and arms control agreements, such as the elimination of intermediate range ballistic missiles, raised questions over the need for SDI. As Pres. George H. Bush took office in 1989, he faced a similar dilemma as Presidents Johnson and Nixon faced more than 20 years before: how to proceed with missile defense given security and political concerns over feasibility, need, and affordability.

SDI was significantly reduced and refocused with the fall of the Berlin Wall and the power of partisan politics. Improving East-West relations eliminated the urgency and rationale for the grand SDI vision. Consequently, the Bush administration sought to preserve the ABM program by changing the focus to prevention of limited or accidental missile attacks against the United States. The new program, global protection against limited strikes (GPALS), was a compromise designed to appease Republicans by continuing work on a missile-defense system while reducing the scope and cost to placate Democrats.

The GPALS program enjoyed a brief period of optimism but soon faded under the tyranny of domestic politics. In October 1991, Premier Mikhail S. Gorbachev proposed a joint US-Soviet defense system as part of the Strategic Arms Reduction Treaty (START) II discussions. This proposal received bipartisan congressional support and was followed by passage of the Missile Defense Act of 1991.[12] This act directed the president to seek amendments to the 1972 ABM Treaty and to field a treaty-compliant defense system by 1996. In 1992, Russian president Boris Yeltsin and President Bush agreed to parameters for START II as well as committing to cooperation on a Global Protection System. Unfortunately, the short-lived consensus on missile defense was derailed by the US recession which turned US attention to domestic issues and a demand for a "peace dividend" through reduced defense spending. This focus on domestic issues was a key contributor to President Clinton's successful election. Moreover, the collapse of the Soviet Union left Russia in disarray and soured US-Russian relations which curtailed pursuit of a joint missile-defense effort. As a result of the ascending primacy of domestic politics, missile defense was dealt a tremendous setback as President Clinton took office in 1993.

President Clinton and Defense Secretary Les Aspin initiated the "Bottom Up Review" (BUR), which resulted in radical change to the missile-defense program. The BUR slashed funding for missile defense from $39 billion over the next five years to $18 billion. In addition, the BUR placed top priority on theater as opposed to national missile defense (NMD) with the additional caveat that all systems remain compliant with the 1972 ABM Treaty. As Secretary Aspin famously stated, "We're taking the 'Star' out of Star Wars." This effectively reduced work on space-based sensors and interceptors to basic research and development. In traditional fashion, Aspin also made a name change as the Strategic Defense Initiative received the more subdued moniker of the Ballistic Missile Defense Organization (BMDO).[13]

Current Era of Missile Defense

Just as domestic politics signaled a downturn in NMD in 1992, the "Republican Revolution" of 1994 along with security issues in Asia resuscitated the program. One of the planks of Newt Gingrich's Contract with America was a clarion call for "renewing America's commitment to an effective national missile defense."[14] The Contract with America was highly influential and gave the Republicans leverage to cast Democrats as soft on defense and unconcerned with national security. Much as Johnson had done 30 years prior, the Clinton administration offered up a missile-defense compromise to diffuse political criticism. In 1996 the "three-plus-three" approach was unveiled, which committed the US to three more years of NMD research, and then a deployment decision based on cost, technical maturity, and security needs. A system could then be fielded three years later if all factors favored deploying the system.

In 1998 a series of events put missile defense on the front page and set the stage for the Missile Defense Act of 1999. The first event was the release of the Welch panel findings, which severely criticized the technical feasibility and planning for the "three-plus-three" program. Citing numerous delays, overruns, and test failures in theater systems, the report called the BMDO plan to field an NMD system a "rush to failure."[15] The Welch report was initially a big blow to missile-defense advocates, but their hopes were revived later in the summer by release of the Rumsfeld commission report on the ballistic-missile threat to the United States.[16]

The Rumsfeld report was highly critical of available intelligence estimates predicting 15 years before rogue nations would develop long-range ballistic missiles. The report highlighted flaws and deficiencies in US intelligence practices and predicted countries such as North Korea or Iran could obtain credible missile capability in only five years.[17] Released on 15 July 1998, the Rumsfeld report was immediately validated by the launch

13

of an Iranian medium-ranged missile a week later.[18] The crowning confirmation occurred in August when North Korea unexpectedly launched a three-stage Taepo Dong I missile theoretically capable of reaching Alaska or Hawaii. Subsequent analysis determined North Korea could possibly attack the continental United States if it added a third stage to its larger Taepo Dong II missile.[19]

The combination of the Welch and Rumsfeld reports with Asian ballistic-missile proliferation reinvigorated funding and urgency for missile defense. While the Welch report initially hurt missile-defense advocates, it also highlighted issues in funding and priority, which called into question the Clinton administration's sincerity to the "three-plus-three" plan. Indeed, within six months Defense Secretary William S. Cohen added $6 billion to the NMD program.[20] Moreover, the newfound missile-defense urgency led to the passage of the Missile Defense Act of 1999 which states: "It is the policy of the United States to deploy as soon as is technologically possible an effective NMD system capable of defending the territory of the United States against limited ballistic missile attack (whether accidental, unauthorized, or deliberate) with funding subject to the annual authorization of appropriations and the annual appropriation of funds for NMD."[21] Thus, as the Clinton administration left office in 2001, the fortunes of NMD turned from precipitous decline to new life with a mandate for limited defense against ballistic-missile attack.

The Bush administration entered office with sincere intentions to field an NMD and acted to overcome hedges from the Clinton administration. The first obstacle to go was the 1972 ABM Treaty. The Clinton administration sought desperately to find a politically acceptable missile-defense position that would be compliant with the ABM Treaty. The fear was that abrogating the ABM Treaty would derail arms control and counter-proliferation efforts with Russia. However, the treaty's limitations on sensor and launcher locations were intentionally designed to reduce the effectiveness of ABM systems. For example, the ABM Treaty did not allow sea- or space-based interceptors. In addition, the treaty did not permit missile tracking sensors to be widely separated from the missile launcher. This limits the effective range of the system as sensors need to be close to the threat in order to maximize response time. Consequently, even a limited NMD was not feasible within the bounds of an un-modified ABM Treaty. The Bush administration was unable to reach an agreement with Russia on a modified ABM Treaty and consequently withdrew from the accord in 2002.

The elimination of the ABM Treaty enabled rethinking of stra-tegic deterrence theory and doctrine. The US goals for originally signing the ABM Treaty in 1972 were no longer compelling in 2002. The Soviet Union was irreversibly disintegrated, and the US and Russia were significantly decreasing nuclear arsenals. Moreover, the emerging ballistic-missile threat does not share the same characteristics as the Soviet Union. The Soviet Union was a single, well-known, strategically stable, and rational op-ponent. The modern threat is diverse, difficult to understand, unpredictable, and often irrational. As a result, the radically new threat required a new approach to strategic security policy. Just as the Air Force transformed from a Cold War construct of strategic and tactical forces to expeditionary forces, the Bush administration embraced a fundamental change in the con-struct for strategic deterrence as described in the 2001 *Nuclear Posture Review* (*NPR*).

The *NPR* unveiled the most significant shift in US strategic nuclear policy since the end of the Cold War. The *NPR* estab-lished a new triad of strategic and conventional strike forces, missile defenses, and responsive infrastructure to replace the Cold War triad of ICBMs, SLBMs, and bombers. The *NPR* also represents the most serious attempt in US history to formally integrate NMD into US strategic policy. Indeed, the 2001 *NPR* was followed by *National Security Presidential Directive 23/ NSPD-23: National Policy on Ballistic Missile Defense* which is a clear and strong affirmation of the importance of missile de-fense: "The new strategic challenges of the 21st century require us to think differently, but they also require us to act. The de-ployment of effective missile defenses is an essential element of the United States' broader efforts to transform our defense and deterrence policies and capabilities to meet the new threats we face. Defending the American people against these new threats is my highest priority as commander in chief, and the highest priority of my Administration."[22]

15

Although the wars in Iraq and Afghanistan pushed missile defense out of the limelight, the Bush administration continues strong support for the missile-defense program. In keeping with tradition, the Bush administration changed the name of the BMDO to the Missile Defense Agency (MDA) in 2002 giving the organization more status as a declared Department of Defense (DOD) agency. More importantly, funding for the missile-defense program was significantly increased and was near $8 billion in 2006 with over $10 billion requested for 2007.[23] Progress on fielding the first ICBM defense system is proceeding with a rudimentary system currently in place that is available in case of national emergency.[24] A suite of additional capabilities are in development and will be incrementally fielded over the next decade.

Conclusion

The US missile-defense legacy reveals several common threads that shed light on the ongoing debate. First, missile defense is strongly impacted by domestic and partisan politics. The role of domestic politics is clear as missile defense has been alternately nurtured or reviled as much for political gain as for military effectiveness. Every decision to field a missile-defense system prior to 2001 was heavily motivated by partisan politics as exemplified by President Johnson's Sentinel program, President Clinton's "three-plus-three" effort, and President Bush's GPALS system.

Second, international politics also strongly influence missile-defense programs. For example, the relationship with Russia and China drove the Cold War arms races resulting in a nuclear standoff, acceptance of assured destruction, and the 1972 ABM Treaty that temporarily ended missile-defense efforts. The influence of international diplomacy is readily evident in declassified memos written during the ABM Treaty negotiations such as this excerpt from President Nixon to the lead US negotiator explaining why the United States agreed to allow two ABM sites: "It is my conclusion that pressing for a complete ban on ABMs would risk jeopardizing the understanding already achieved with the USSR. This is all the more true because if we went to a zero ABM proposal we would have to ask for more sweeping offensive limitations than seem immediately negotiable. Our

16

objective should be to consolidate gains we have made, and translate our mutual commitment into a viable agreement."[25]

Moreover, missile-defense systems have a legacy of long development cycles as a result of perturbations from politics, international security considerations, and the immense technical challenge. The long development cycle leads to faster change in the strategic environment and in the threat than technology can adapt to resulting in poor cost versus benefit assessments. For example, the Cold War Sentinel and Safeguard systems were rendered obsolete by the rapid buildup of ICBMs. Likewise, the need for Star Wars succumbed to the end of the Cold War effectively ending the second era of missile defense. The current systems were also hampered until 2002 by political mandates to abide by the limits of the 1972 ABM Treaty. This politically driven limitation is one of the key reasons leap-ahead missile technologies did not advance beyond research and development in the late 1980s and 1990s. Consequently, history suggests that the next system needs to (1) correctly anticipate the future threat and (2) focus on systems and technology that can be deployed in time to make a difference.

Finally, the history of the debate over NMD shares much in common with the debate over WMD with one critical difference—lack of an intellectual consensus on technical feasibility. While there is much debate over the use of nuclear weapons, there is little argument over whether a nuclear weapon will function as designed. Clearly, the long legacy of use from the Manhattan Project, Hiroshima and Nagasaki, and decades of testing has put to rest questions of technical feasibility for nuclear weapons. On the other hand, a common thread through the half-century debate on missile defense is the crippling lack of consensus on the technical feasibility and cost of an effective NMD. Missile-defense systems have an inconsistent record of performance in testing and many fundamental questions remain. In order to address this issue more closely, chapter 3 describes and analyzes the status and likely technical effectiveness of the current US NMD program.

Notes

1. Yanarella, *Missile Defense Controversy*, 70–82.

17

2. *Wikipedia*, "Starfish Prime," http://en.wikipedia.org/wiki/Starfish_Prime.
3. Prof. Theodore Postol, MIT, interview by the author, October 2005.
4. Graham, *Hit to Kill*, 6–7.
5. Ibid, 5.
6. Ibid, 7.
7. Federation of American Scientists (FAS), "China's Nuclear Force."
8. Graham, *Hit to Kill*, 7–8.
9. Burr, *Missile Defense Thirty Years Ago*.
10. Union of Concerned Scientists (UCSUSA), *Missile Defense*.
11. Graham, *Hit to Kill*, 15.
12. Ibid, 20–21.
13. Missile Defense Agency, "History of Ballistic Missile Defense."
14. US House, *Republican Contract*.
15. FAS, *Report of the Panel on Reducing Risk*.
16. FAS, *Executive Summary*.
17. Ibid.
18. Katzman, *Iran*.
19. Graham, *Hit to Kill*, 64.
20. Missile Defense Agency, "History of Ballistic Missile Defense."
21. Ibid.
22. FAS, *National Security*.
23. Roosevelt, "MDA Requests."
24. Butler, "Boosting Confidence."
25. Burr, ed., *Missile Defense Thirty Years Ago*.

Chapter 3

Evaluation of Current National Missile-Defense Programs

The new strategic challenges of the 21st century require us to think differently, but they also require us to act. The deployment of effective missile defenses is an essential element of the United States' broader efforts to transform our defense and deterrence policies and capabilities to meet the new threats we face. Defending the American people against these new threats is my highest priority as Commander in Chief, and the highest priority of my Administration.

—Pres. George W. Bush
NSPD-23

The current missile-defense effort is the most comprehensive attempt by the United States to field a national BMD system. The US missile-defense program is managed by the MDA with specific guidance from the president and secretary of defense. The MDA translated the strategic objectives into a portfolio of systems and technology programs designed to field an effective missile-defense system. The following sections discuss the overall strategy, the MDA's suite of programs, and an analysis of how well the effort is proceeding.

The Current Strategy

National Security Presidential Directive 23 lays out the US commitment to fielding a limited defense as well as provides goals and guidelines for implementation. The goal of the missile-defense program is to be a contributing element of the new triad of strategic forces including nuclear and conventional strike forces, strategic defense, and responsive infrastructure. The specific goals for the missile-defense system are to

- assure allies and friends that the United States will not be coerced by missile threats,

19

- dissuade potential adversaries from investing in ballistic missiles,

- deter ballistic missile use by denying benefits of any attack, and

- defend against ballistic missiles should deterrence fail.[1]

Another major goal of the missile-defense program is to enable US cooperation with friends and allies: "The threats of the 21st century also endanger our friends and allies around the world, it is essential that we work together to defend against these threats. Missile-defense cooperation will be a feature of U.S. relations with close, long-standing allies, and an important means to build new relationships with new friends like Russia."[2]

Presidential guidance also directs the secretary of defense to implement an evolutionary acquisition strategy:

> The Defense Department plans to employ an evolutionary approach to the development and deployment of missile defenses to improve our defenses over time. The United States will not have a final, fixed missile defense architecture. Rather, we will deploy an initial set of capabilities that will evolve to meet the changing threat and to take advantage of technological developments. The composition of missile defenses, to include the number and location of systems deployed, will change over time.[3]

The MDA is charged with implementing the evolutionary acquisition policy and fielding the US ballistic missile-defense system. The MDA's plan to fulfill its mission is to develop and deploy a nonnuclear, layered defense against ballistic missiles by delivering capability in two-year blocks. The first block increment occurred in 2004 through 2005 (Block 04) and will be followed in two years by a Block 06 update. Block 04 provides an initial defensive capability for the United States against North Korean long-range missiles while providing protection for deployed forces from theater ballistic missiles (TBM).[4] Block 06 seeks to add protection from long-range threats from the Middle East while expanding coverage of allies and improving capability against countermeasures. New sensors, interceptors, and response to the changing threat are planned for Blocks 08 and beyond.

Another aspect of the MDA's implementation strategy is to develop and deploy primarily ground-based hit-to-kill interceptors that use kinetic impact or directed energy to destroy incoming missiles. Previous missile-defense systems such as the US Spartan, Sprint, and the Soviet Galosh systems used nuclear warheads. Nuclear warheads are effective, but potential collateral damage and political costs of nuclear-tipped interceptors lead to a preference for conventional kill technology. In addition, the United States has stepped back from deploying space-based interceptors due to the technical immaturity and high political and economic costs of space-based weapons. Hit-to-kill technology is rapidly maturing, but there are many challenges remaining including basing options, engaging targets in a realistic environment, and fielding an integrated command-and-control system.

Missile Engagement Regimes

The MDA's layered defense is based on engaging threat missiles in one or more of the three phases of missile flight: boost, midcourse, or terminal. The first phase of missile flyout is the boost phase, which is defined as the period from launch until the booster burns out. The boost phase is typically very short with a maximum duration of five to six minutes for long-range, liquid-fueled ICBMs. The midcourse phase consists of the period of flight beginning with booster cutoff and ending with reentry into the atmosphere. Thus, the midcourse phase includes the majority of the exoatmospheric flight. This is also usually the longest phase of a ballistic missile's flight (~30 minutes) but can vary dramatically depending on flight profile and range. The final segment of a missile's trajectory is the terminal phase which lasts from reentry until surface impact. The MDA's layered approach consists of developing systems to attack ballistic missiles in the different phases to maximize flexibility and increase the probability of kill by allowing multiple engagements.

Each of these regimes has significant advantages as well as technical and political challenges. For example, some advantages of boost-phase intercept (BPI) are the ability to defend large areas with a small deployment footprint and a low likelihood of encountering deceptive countermeasures. Conversely, the ability to go through the entire kill chain in a few minutes and intercept a ballistic missile is a daunting technical challenge coupled with political issues of basing, situational awareness, and consequence management. Likewise, midcourse and terminal defense strategies have associated strengths and weaknesses that must be understood to make a sound assessment. The following sections will describe the various systems in development by engagement regime. The evaluations will focus primarily on the interceptors since the various layers use essentially the same sensor network and centralized command-and-control system.

Boost-Phase Defense Systems

The MDA's current BPI elements are the airborne laser (ABL) and the kinetic energy interceptor (KEI). The ABL is the MDA's baseline boost-phase system and consists of a high-powered chemical laser mounted in a Boeing 747 aircraft. The ABL concept is to destroy missiles by lasing a hole in the booster, inducing failure and resulting in the warhead falling short of its intended target. Hypothetical estimates for maximum effective range vary from 300 kilometers (km) against solid-fuel rockets to around 600 km for thin-skinned, liquid-fueled boosters.[5] In December 2005, the "first light" test was successfully accomplished in a ground facility and demonstrated the ability of the laser to achieve the desired power output. The MDA will next integrate the laser into the Boeing 747 with hopes of a live-fire test against a target missile in 2008. As mentioned previously, the boost phase is relatively short; consequently, the ABL must be in-theater, airborne, and able to quickly maneuver into position to be effective. The MDA anticipates that a fleet of seven aircraft will enable at least two aircraft to be airborne 24/7 to patrol a designated area.[6]

The ABL has suffered significant cost and schedule delays leading the MDA to establish the KEI system as an alternative boost-phase concept. The goal of the KEI system is to develop a sea- or ground-launched missile with sufficient acceleration to perform BPIs. Extremely high acceleration is required because the boost-phase interceptor must "outrun" the accelerating target missile before the end of the boost phase. The ABL solves this problem with directed energy that travels at the speed of light. Unfortunately, current interceptors do not have enough

USAF Photo

Airborne laser test aircraft

acceleration and maneuverability to effectively perform BPI. The KEI program is investigating new technologies in an attempt to improve booster acceleration.[7] Additionally, KEI breakthroughs will also benefit interceptors designed for midcourse and terminal phase as improved acceleration and maneuverability are critical to all classes of kinetic kill vehicles.[8]

Assessment of Boost-Phase Systems

The proposed BPI systems have many technical and strategic deficiencies and are not likely to be useful to US missile-defense goals in the near term. First, the extremely limited missile-engagement timelines will pose an unacceptable challenge to decision-making and command-and-control systems. The window for the complete event is a maximum of five minutes to include detection, tracking, identification, and then engagement. Indeed, the decision to fire needs to be made in the first few minutes or even seconds in order to have sufficient time for engagement.[9] Investigations into the friendly-fire incidents involving the Patriot missile in Operation Iraqi Freedom (OIF) illustrate the immense difficulty in making the right decision in such a short period with ambiguous information. In OIF these pressures conspired to cost the lives of aircrew when a missile operator launched a missile based on conflicting data.[10] The stakes for error in BPI are possibly even higher given the potential for a nuclear, biological, or chemical warhead to detonate in an unexpected area thereby requiring extensive consequence management. A BPI engagement will likely result in launching missiles or lasers over foreign soil and will require diplomatic coordination. In the event of a successful intercept, there is the additional worry of collateral damage as BPI systems attack the booster, which means that the warhead is very likely to be undamaged and will continue on an altered path that is difficult to predict. For example, the warhead from a missile launched from North Korea against Washington, DC, could easily land in Canada or the Midwest in the event of a "successful" intercept.

The operational and basing requirements and limited intercept range of BPI systems are also a concern. Operationally, all elements of the complex defense system, such as battle management, command-and-control, and sensors integration, must stay on high alert as any lapse could eliminate the opportunity for an effective intercept. This level of constant readiness is costly and taxing, leading to increased risk of mistakes. In addition, the limited range of BPI systems requires the interceptors to be physically close (several hundred km) from the target which will often require assistance from neighboring countries; but even this does not guarantee success. For example, two ABLs patrolling just outside the borders of Iran would still leave large areas undefended even assuming a generous 500 km range and complete cooperation from all neighboring countries.[11] As illustrated by the recent US eviction from Uzbekistan, basing rights are difficult to achieve and sustain in many areas of the world. Sea-based defenses offer some reprieve but are obviously also limited against inland threats.

Midcourse Systems

Midcourse systems are the focal point of the MDA's Block 04 layered-defense strategy against long-range threats. The primary components of the suite of midcourse systems are the Ground-based Midcourse Defense (GMD) system and the sea-based Aegis Ballistic Missile Defense. The GMD system is the first element to reach limited defensive operations (LDO) status and is currently focused on deterring missile launch from North Korea. The GMD system consists of a network of sensors, ground-based interceptors, and battle management systems. Defense Support Program (DSP) satellites provide launch detection and early warning. An array of radars distributed throughout the Pacific and West Coast provide tracking and guidance data to the ground-based interceptors (GBI) located at Fort Greely, Alaska, with an additional complement of GBIs based at Vandenburg AFB, California.

MDA Photo

Launch of ground-based interceptor

The GBI are multistage missiles that place a maneuverable exoatmoshpheric kill vehicle (EKV) on a trajectory to intercept the target missile. After separation from the booster, the EKV acquires the threat missile with an onboard seeker and then maneuvers to an intercept point to destroy the target. The entire enterprise, including fire control and battle management for the GMD system, is coordinated by the Joint National Integration Center at Schriever AFB, Colorado.

Navy Photo

Launch of standard missile-3 from an Aegis BMD cruiser

The Aegis BMD is a ship-based BMD system consisting of upgrades to the existing Aegis-class vessels to enable mid-course and terminal missile defense. The Aegis BMD is one of the most versatile elements of the US missile-defense arsenal as it is highly mobile, has a very effective radar sensor, and employs an advanced interceptor. The system is capable of tracking and engaging short-range ballistic missiles (<1,000 km) (SRBM) and medium-range ballistic missiles (1,000–3,000 km) (MRBM) autonomously or can be used as a sensor or shooter as part of a larger "system-of-systems" construct. For example, the upgraded Aegis radar recently demonstrated the ability to track ICBM-class targets as part of the network supporting the GMD system.[12] Aegis also employs an upgraded standard missile (SM-3) that delivers a maneuverable kinetic kill vehicle capable of intercepting targets in the upper atmosphere or even in low exoatmospheric conditions. The MDA plans to incrementally modify Aegis ships to perform the missile-defense function with 12 ships planned to be available as part of Block 04 with additional ships upgraded to the BMD role in subsequent blocks.[13]

Assessment of the MDA Midcourse Systems

The MDA's midcourse systems have limitations and challenges but are making progress. First, the basing requirements are less demanding than either boost- or terminal-phase systems. It is possible to defend the entire United States from North Korea and Iran with only three interceptor sites, which can be located well away from the threat country. The addition of a third site in Europe to the operational GMD interceptor sites in Alaska and California would accomplish this goal.[14] Moreover, the flexibility in locating interceptor sites allows decision makers to maximize the deterrence value of the system without undesired provocation such as basing an ABL on Iran's borders. In addition, ground-based missiles are much easier to keep on 24/7 alert than air- or sea-based interceptors providing a more credible and persistent defense.

Finally, the GMD allows the best opportunity for near-term defense against long-range ballistic missiles. The GMD system builds on the legacy of 20-plus years and $100 billion of NMD investment since the 1980s. Hit–to-kill technology has had many bumps in the road, but the systems which comprise the GMD have demonstrated a limited level of capability that should not be casually dismissed. Furthermore, the GMD architecture incorporates existing assets, such as the nation's suite of early warning radars, and has "hooks" to accept new systems and technology. Thus, the GMD system has many of the characteristics sought in *NSPD-23*, but there are substantial issues.

A major criticism of the GMD system is the vulnerability to countermeasures. Countermeasures against a midcourse defense system are relatively easy to conceive, design, and implement. One reason for this is the lack of atmospheric drag during midcourse flight. The lack of drag allows countermeasures, such as chaff or decoys, to travel at the same speed and along the same trajectory as the warhead. The close proximity of the countermeasures to the warhead makes it difficult for radar to distinguish between the warhead, debris from launch, and the decoys. Ground-based sensors can at best guide the kill vehicle to a cloud of targets of which only one may be the warhead. Thus, the kill vehicle must perform its own target discrimination with onboard sensors while moving at incredibly fast-closing velocities of up to 10 km per *second*, which is literally faster than a speeding bullet.[15] Even the slightest error can cause the kill vehicle to miss, and six inches equals a mile in the hit-to-kill scenario.

The kill vehicle's onboard systems are also susceptible to decoys and countermeasures due to the fast closure rates and a limited field of view. The GMD and Aegis interceptors use passive infrared (IR) sensors and discrimination algorithms to identify the warhead and then guide the kill vehicle on a collision course. IR sensors are used due to their small size, which allows them to fit in the kill vehicle and the ability to passively detect the thermal signature of the warhead and other objects in the threat cloud. In addition, optical trackers such as the kill vehicle's IR system provide very accurate angle tracking data that is needed for a direct hit.

Onboard algorithms sort through the IR data and attempt to identify the warhead by looking for specific thermal features. This is one of the most difficult tasks for the kill vehicle as decoys can easily duplicate or mask the IR signature of the warhead.[16] Moreover, while the small size allows the IR sensor to fit

MDA Photo

GMD exoatmospheric kill vehicle

in the kill vehicle, the downside is that it does not have very high resolution. The small IR focal plane will initially only see an amorphous thermal cloud and will not be able to distinguish between individual objects until moments before impact. Consequently, the kill vehicle is very susceptible to countermeasures because it has little opportunity to react, limited field of view and resolution, and must quickly home in on an object in the threat cloud with limited external guidance.

The MDA recognizes the countermeasure challenge and is developing a set of techniques to improve the discrimination capability of the kill vehicles. Specific techniques and data are classified, but the overall thrust is to increase the ability and opportunity of the kill vehicle to correctly identify the warhead prior to having to commit to intercept. One obvious solution is to launch multiple kill vehicles at a single target. The current plan is to launch salvos of multiple interceptors per target.[17] Furthermore, the MDA initiated the multiple kill-vehicle program to investigate placing two or more kill vehicles on a single interceptor. This would greatly enhance the opportunity for the kill vehicles to approach from slightly different aspect angles or concentrate on different targets to improve the likelihood of identifying the warhead. Other efforts include improvement to focal plane resolution or IR frequency response to increase the distance at which the kill vehicle can reliably identify the warhead.[18] These efforts will improve the capability of the GMD system against simple decoys, but a responsive adversary could introduce more sophisticated countermeasures necessitating an ongoing commitment to improved target discrimination.

Other major criticisms of the GMD system include test failures and the lack of realistic testing. The GMD system has a checkered history of flight-test results as the Government Accounting Office reports only seven successful intercepts in 18 attempts since the 1980s.[19] The sources of failure include kill-vehicle hardware and software errors, target launch issues, and booster launch issues with no discernable pattern. Moreover, most of the testing to date has been of a developmental nature, which makes it difficult to determine the operational utility of the system. Future tests are designed to incorporate more operational equipment and personnel, threat representative targets, and more challenging scenarios to improve test realism.

Terminal-Phase Systems

The MDA's terminal defense interceptor portfolio relies mainly on theater missile defense developed by the services. The current list of systems includes the Army's Patriot advanced capabilities 3 (PAC-3) and terminal high-altitude area defense (THAAD) as well as the Navy's Aegis BMD system. These systems have the most maturity since they have been in development for decades by the services for the air defense mission. Multiple versions of the Patriot were used in the Gulf War with mixed results. Claims of successful intercepts by the Patriot PAC-2 (proximity warhead) against Iraqi Scuds in Desert Storm have been largely disproved.[20] However, the PAC-3 and its new hit-to-kill interceptor performed far better in OIF although some of the luster was marred by tragic friendly-fire incidents against allied aircraft.

MDA Photo

Patriot (PAC-3) missile launch

Assessment of Terminal-Defense Systems

Terminal-phase missile defense can only protect a limited area as compared to boost-phase or midcourse systems. The high speed and steep attack angle of incoming warheads in the terminal phase requires the interceptors to be based near the protected target. Hence, a large and costly number of terminal-defense systems are needed to protect a large area such as the continental United States. There are no plans or requirements to permanently base terminal defenses on US territory to defend population centers or military targets. The MDA's command-and-control system is designed to integrate these systems into the national command structure to support use in protecting deployed forces or overseas allies should the need arise. Consequently, the terminal missile-defense systems available to the MDA represent primarily a theater military capability which will not play a central role in countering long-range missile attack against the United States.

However, terminal-defensive systems have a critical role internationally due to the wide proliferation and use of shorter-range ballistic missiles on a global scale. Moreover, these systems are vital to defending our deployed forces and allies. *NSPD-23* recognizes this fact by stating that "The terms 'theater' and 'national' are interchangeable depending on the circumstances, and thus are not meaningful ways of categorizing missile defenses. For example, some of the systems being pursued by the United States to protect deployed forces are capable of defending the entire national territory of some friends and allies, thereby meeting the definition of a 'national' missile-defense system."[21] From World War II to OIF, SRBMs have been used in combat and will almost certainly be used in future conflicts as SRBM technology is readily available to any rogue state or even nonstate actor. Moreover, there is an emerging global norm accepting the use of conventionally armed TBMs.[22] Consequently, terminal-phase systems may not be the primary means of defending the US mainland, but these systems often drive strategic missile-defense policy because of their immense operational military value and importance to allies.

Conclusion

The ability of the US missile-defense program to achieve all of the technical performance goals outlined in *NSPD-23* remains uncertain. The ability to defend the homeland against long-range attack is a difficult technical challenge, and the current missile-defense capability is indeed limited. However, defense against short- and medium-range missiles is showing promise, which is critical since these systems were needed in the past and are the most likely to be called upon again to defend US interests and allies abroad.

The baseline boost-phase system, the airborne laser, has experienced severe cost overruns and delays and will not conduct an airborne live-fire test until 2008 at the earliest. Moreover, basing issues, limited operational persistence, and extremely short response timelines cloud the missile-defense utility of the ABL even if the technology issues are solved. Funding for the KEI program has repeatedly been cut leaving doubt that a ground- or sea-based BPI system can be fielded in the near term.[23]

The GMD system is the centerpiece of the MDA's near-term missile defense against long-range missiles and provides the best hope for a credible, albeit limited, capability against this class of threat. The GMD has the flexible basing and persistent operation necessary to defend against a surprise attack. In addition, many elements of the GMD are technically mature with all key elements having at least been demonstrated in flight testing. The downside of the GMD is the susceptibility to countermeasures and an uneven record of success in developmental testing. Hence, the GMD is not likely to provide a foolproof defense against tens of hostile missiles with countermeasures in the near term but may be able to deter and defeat a more limited long-range attack against the United States by ICBMs without countermeasures.

The terminal-defense systems are the most technically mature and show promise for defending against short- and medium-range ballistic-missile attack. These systems can be integrated into the national missile-defense system to provide additional capability. The improving success of the Patriot PAC-3 and Aegis BMD demonstrate that after decades of development, these systems are approaching an acceptable level of operational utility and are the best hope for international defense and cooperation.

The technical maturity and likely effectiveness of the planned US missile-defense system is a critical factor in evaluating the overall impact on national security and international relations. As a vital part of the new strategic triad, ballistic missile defense has high political and diplomatic value separate from combat use. Hence, missile-defense systems must have enough technical credibility to assure our allies while deterring and dissuading adversaries and must effectively defend US interests when needed. Consequently, unrealistic or false assessment of technical capability and threats can lead to political instability and unnecessary security risks. These concerns are particularly important given the uncertain capability of US missile-defense systems and the considerable impact US missile-defense policy will have on the rest of the world with special emphasis in Asia as discussed in chapter 4.

Notes

1. Jamison, briefing.
2. The White House. "National Policy."
3. Ibid.
4. Obering, address, 9–10.
5. American Physical Society, *Report of the APS Study Group.*
6. Tirpak, "Airborne Laser," 30–34.
7. Barnard, "KEI Now Seen."
8. Ibid.
9. American Physical Society, *Report of the APS Study Group.*
10. Office of the Under Secretary of Defense for Acquisition, Technology, and Logistics, *Report of the Defense Science Board.*
11. American Physical Society, *Report of the APS Study Group.*
12. "Aegis Tracks," *C4I News.*
13. Jamison, briefing.
14. Liang, "Decision on Europe-based GMD Interceptor," 2.
15. American Physical Society, *Report of the APS Study Group.*
16. Garwin, "Holes in the Missile Shield," 70–79.
17. MIT, Lincoln Laboratory, seminar.
18. Congressional Budget Office, *Alternativesfor Boost.*
19. Hildreth, "Kinetic Energy Kill."
20. Kariya, "Patriot's Second Chance," 17–18.
21. FAS, *National Security Presidential Directive.*
22. Feickert, "Missile Survey."
23. Trachtenberg, "Off the Radar," 12–15.

Chapter 4

Asia and the
US Missile-Defense Program

*Japan is the first country in the world to experience terrorism
using chemical gas in an attack in the subways that happened 10 years ago. . . . two-thirds of Japanese supported
the introduction of the Missile Defense system. . . . We hope
the Missile Defense system will contribute greatly to international efforts for countering the proliferation of WMD and its
means of delivery.*

—Mr. Yoshinori Ohno (2004)
Minister of State for
Defense of Japan

*When the Islamic world acquires atomic weapons, the strategy
of the West will hit a dead end—since the use of a single
atomic bomb has the power to destroy Israel completely,
while it will only cause partial damage to the Islamic world.*

—Ayatollah Ali Akbar Hashemi Rafsanjani (2001)
President of Iran (1989–97)

Asia is the continent most impacted by the political and strategic implications of US missile-defense policies for the next
decade. As illustrated in chapter 2, Russia is traditionally a
focus of US missile-defense policy since the end of World War II
and will continue to be a key player. China is viewed as the
emerging peer competitor to the United States and has voiced
definite opinions on US missile-defense policy. Beyond these
two nations, WMD proliferation, rogue states and actors, and
nuclear tensions are also concentrated in Asia. Globally the
trend has been for non-Asian nations to renounce WMD and
ballistic missile aspirations such as Brazil, South Africa, and
Libya. However, Asia contains all of the nations overtly pursuing
nuclear ambitions other than the original five Non-Proliferation
Treaty (NPT) nuclear states: the United States, Great Britain,
France, Russia, and China. Other than the NPT nuclear states,
Israel, North Korea, Iran, Pakistan, and India are the only coun-

tries known or suspected of active nuclear weapons and ballistic missile programs.[1] Table 1 also illustrates that the preponderance of medium- to long-range ballistic-missiles- (or ICBMs with >5,000 km range) wielding states are in Asia. In addition, non-state actors such as al-Qaeda operate in Asia and seek to acquire WMD to find an asymmetric leverage against the United States. The concentration of key strategic actors and issues clearly signifies Asia as a focal point for US missile-defense efforts.

Table 1. Deployed ballistic missiles by type and country

Ballistic-Missile Type and Range	Countries
Intercontinental/Intermediate Range (ICBM/IRBM) (Land- and Sea-based) >3000 km	Known: China, France, Russia, United Kingdom, United States Possible: India, Iran, North Korea
Medium Range 1000–3000 km	Israel, North Korea, Saudi Arabia, China, India, Pakistan, Iran
Short Range 70–1000 km	Afghanistan, Algeria, Argentina, Armenia, Belarus, Bulgaria, China, Czech Republic, Egypt, Greece, India, Iran, Iraq, Israel, Kazakhstan, Libya, Netherlands, North Korea, Pakistan, Romania, Russia, Serbia, Slovakia, South Korea, Syria Taiwan, Turkey, Turkmenistan, Ukraine, United Arab Emirates, Vietnam, and Yemen

Adapted from Joseph Cirincione, "The Declining Ballistic Missile Threat, 2005," *Policy Outlook: Carnegie Non-Proliferation*, February 2005; and Andrew Feickert, "Missile Survey: Ballistic and Cruise Missiles of Foreign Countries," Congressional Research Service, RL30427, 5 March 2004; and Federation of American Scientists, *Unclassified Summary of a National Intelligence Estimate: Foreign Missile Developments and the Ballistic Missile Threat through 2015*, National Intelligence Council, December 2001.

Asia also contains the world's most contentious nuclear-possessing and nuclear-aspiring powers; for example, disputes between North Korea and Japan, China and Taiwan, India and Pakistan, and Iran and the West. The most extensive use of ballistic missiles since World War II has been confined to Asia: some 1,600 Russian TBMs used in Afghanistan, 350 TBMs used in the Iran-Iraq war, and nearly 100 TBMs used by Iraq in the Gulf Wars.[2] Indeed, Asia is the scene of the only use of modern US ABM systems and the near-term focus for the GMD system. Thus, the near-term strategic and political value of the current US missile-defense program will be largely determined by its impact in Asia.

The following sections investigate the influence and role of missile defense on key Asian countries and relationships. Any assessment on missile defense in Asia should surely include the known WMD- and ballistic-missile capable states in Asia which are Russia, China, India, Pakistan, and Israel. In addition North Korea and Iran have demonstrated ballistic-missile capability and are actively pursuing nuclear weapons. Japan is another key actor due to its substantial economic might and growing assertiveness in military affairs. Asian-based nonstate actors, such as al-Qaeda and transnational corporations, also impact US missile-defense policy.

Russia

Since the breakup of the Soviet Union, the relationship between Russia and the United States on missile defense has moved from optimistic to suspicious. Early in the 1990s there was a brief period of hope for genuine missile-defense cooperation between Russia and the United States as the two countries investigated possible modifications to the 1972 ABM Treaty and even explored a joint missile-defense system. However, Russia's ability and later desire to continue with these initiatives waned as the country plunged into disarray.

The late 1990s were a disaster for Russia and its military leading to increasing tension with the United States. Boris Yeltsin and other Russian civilian leaders were fearful of the military following the coup attempt in 1991. Consequently, few resources were provided to the Russian military in an effort to keep the generals weak and amenable to civilian control.[3] There was a precipitous decline in military funding and an 80 percent reduction in manpower along with tremendous chaos and corruption. Unfortunately, the "shock therapy" attempt to convert Russia into a Western-style democracy and market-based economy failed miserably. By the time Pres. Vladimir Putin assumed office in 2000, the general Russian population, and especially the military, had soured on further cooperation with the West. Indeed, by 2001 a majority of Russians believed the United States was not a country that could be trusted and had intentionally tried to subvert their nation with predatory economic policies.[4] Hence, President Putin has steered Russia on an increasingly independent course from the West resulting in decreased cooperation for missile defense.

Current Position and Policy Drivers

Russia has publicly taken a "wait and see" and dismissive posture in response to recent US missile-defense policy; however, closer review of Russian military strategy and commentary reveals concern. Russia's conventional forces retain only a fraction of their Soviet-era capability. The poor military performance in Chechnya is an example of how far the conventional forces have fallen. Russian military leaders are quite aware of the prowess demonstrated by allied conventional forces in Iraq, Afghanistan, and the Balkans. As a result, Russia now leans heavily on its vast nuclear arsenal for deterrence as it attempts to transform its Soviet-era army into a more capable, professional force similar to Western militaries.[5] Moreover, Russia is not enamored with US plans to deploy missile defense, as this directly threatens its nuclear deterrence which is the foundation of Russian national security and a cornerstone of Russia's struggle to retain world-power status.[6]

Russian leaders remain skeptical of US pledges that the current missile defense is only targeted against rogue states as demonstrated by several actions. Russian deputy prime minister Sergei Ivanov outlined Russia's commitment to its nuclear forces in a January 2006 *Wall Street Journal* article: "Russia does not intend to give up its nuclear capability, as it is still a key deterrent and a crucial instrument in protecting our national interests and achieving certain political objectives."[7]

In order to preserve the effectiveness of its nuclear deterrence, Russia is developing new ICBMs, the Bulava and Topol-M, with maneuvering warheads specifically designed to defeat missile-defense systems.[8] Russia also withdrew from the START II Treaty following US withdrawal from the ABM Treaty in 2002. As a result, Russia continues to maintain a significant force of multiple warhead missiles dealing a blow to years of nuclear-arms-reduction negotiations. Russian cooperation in programs, such as the Nunn-Lugar Cooperative Threat Reduction (CTR) program, has cooled as well.[9] Indeed, Russia is generally threatened by US missile-defense plans and is increasingly charting an independent course for its national security.

Likely Future Response

Russia's opinion of the US missile-defense program is not likely to change unless the United States begins to significantly expand the GMD system or weaponize space, at that point the relationship will worsen. Russia tolerates the current US missile-defense program because it still retains a large nuclear arsenal that can easily overwhelm the intentionally limited US system. Moreover, Russian leaders believe their new missiles have countermeasures that should be effective against the nascent US capability, and they are even threatening to reintroduce IRBMs if necessary to maintain the strategic balance.[10] Russia also continues to operate its own BMD system which further mutes criticism of US efforts to field a limited ABM system. Even a reduction or the elimination of the US missile-defense system is not likely to improve US-Russian relationships, as the current cooling in friendly interactions is driven by several unrelated issues. Some of these issues include competing interests in Central Asia, NATO expansion, renewed competition in arms exports, Russia's slide away from democracy, and growing Russian concern over perceived US imperialism.

An area which does bear special attention is the impact of missile-defense policy on future counterproliferation efforts with Russia. Stopping the flow of WMD at the source is widely acknowledged as the best way to combat the use of nuclear weapons by terrorists and rogue states.[11] Moreover, counterproliferation is one of the few remaining areas where US and Russian national interests overlap and continued cooperation is necessary. The cooperative threat reduction program between the United States and Russia has effectively reprocessed 500 tons of weapons grade material which is equivalent to 10,000 warheads.[12] However, this is only half the currently known material. In addition, more material will need to be safely disposed as US and Russian stockpiles draw down to the 2002 Moscow Treaty limits.

Unfortunately, the relationship between the United States and Russia is deteriorating as Russia becomes more independent and assertive. A March 2006 report from the influential Council on Foreign Relations suggests that the very idea of a "strategic partnership" between the United States and Russia no longer seems realistic in the near term.[13] The report recommends that the United States reevaluate foreign policy towards Russia in order to improve relations in the long term. An example of the difficulty is that while the United States and Russia are allegedly partners in dissuading proliferation of nuclear technology in Iran, Russia is quietly selling Iran $1 billion worth of air defense missiles in anticipation of a possible US invasion.[14] Consequently, US decision makers must consider missile defense, counterproliferation, and many other issues within the framework of a complicated and increasingly adversarial relationship with Russia.

China

During the Cold War, China was the secondary focus of US missile-defense efforts after the Soviet Union. Unlike the United States and Soviet Union, China adopted a strategic policy of minimum deterrence much in the fashion endorsed by the Waltz school of strategic thought (after Kenneth N. Waltz) that considers overwhelming nuclear force unnecessary to prevent attack.[15] Consequently, China fielded a small ICBM force of 20–30 missiles under the belief that this was sufficient to deter US or Soviet aggression without the huge expense and excesses of nuclear parity. Not surprisingly, China was one of the most vocal critics of US withdrawal from the 1972 ABM Treaty.[16] Even though China was not a signatory nation, Chinese deterrence was predicated on US vulnerability to long range missile attack under the pretext that even one nuclear weapon landing on a US city was sufficient deterrence.

Since the end of the Cold War, US-Chinese relations have become increasingly complex. On one hand, trade and economic interactions between the two countries has expanded dramatically and is critically important to both countries. China's economy will soon eclipse Great Britain as the fourth largest in the world partially due to increasing trade with foreign partners like the United States.[17] Chinese leaders have intentionally nurtured economic growth in order to avoid a Soviet-style collapse.

Despite the mutually beneficial economic relationship, significant tension remains between the two nations. First, the issue of Taiwan's independence creates persistent friction as the United States walks a fine line between protecting Taiwan from Chinese occupation and maintaining the "one China" policy. Second, China aspires to regional hegemony in Asia that creates direct competition with the United States which has similar aspirations. Furthermore, the United States increasingly identifies China as an emerging peer competitor militarily and economically, as China has five times the US population and an economy growing two to three times faster than the US economy.[18] Events, such as the Chinese response to the US bombing of the Chinese embassy in Belgrade and the US response to the P-3 Orion mishap, highlight the latent tension in the US-Chinese relationship.

Current Position

The two current missile-defense-policy drivers for China are maintaining control of Taiwan and strategic deterrence. China has dramatically increased its arsenal of SRBMs and MRBMs with many of them arrayed to deter Taiwan from thoughts of independence. China currently has an estimated 700 TBMs deployed against Taiwan and is expected to add an additional 75–120 TBMs per year.[19] Chinese doctrine is to use "active defense" to protect its interests in Taiwan by preemptively attacking and overwhelming any possible US defense of the island through sheer numbers.[20] In addition, China has voiced opposition to sale or deployment of Patriot PAC-3 or the Aegis BMD systems to Taiwan and even Japan, as this would threaten a vital national interest and its "active defense" doctrine. A Chinese foreign ministry spokesman recently stated that the sale of theater missiles defense systems to Taiwan "would undermine national security and the unification of China and harm relations between the United States and China."[21]

China is also committed to maintaining an acceptable nuclear deterrence against US aggression. Chinese leaders felt bullied by US threats of nuclear attack in the Korean War and committed to maintaining a credible deterrent to US nuclear forces as a cornerstone of Chinese security.[22] The awesome displays of US conventional forces in the past decade combined with the decision to field a missile-defense system motivated China's current investment in its long-range missile force. China is expanding and improving its arsenal of ICBMs to include fielding of the mobile, solid-fuel DF-31, which is a significant improvement over previous generation missiles. Experts estimate China will increase its ICBM force from the current 20–30 missiles to anywhere from 75 to 100 missiles.[23] Further escalation is anticipated in proportion to the size and capability of the United States, Japanese, and Taiwanese missile-defense capability.

Likely Future Response

Much like Russia, China's response to the planned US missile-defense system is not likely to change in the near future unless there is significant escalation in the numbers of deployed missiles or a push to weaponize space. Deployment of US missile-defense systems to Taiwan and Japan will likely be met with a correlated increase in deployed missiles. Furthermore, China's leaders have clearly articulated that placing interceptors in space will create a strong negative response.[24] Moreover, the cancellation of the planned US missile-defense system will not stop China's missile buildup, as China was already committed to massive military modernization prior to the current US missile-defense effort. Indeed, the buildup started during the Clinton administration *before* the Missile Defense Act of 1999.[25] China planned a 15 percent increase in defense spending in 2006 in large part due to Taiwan's politically provocative actions such as dissolving the government organization responsible for reunification with the mainland.[26] Thus, China's tangible response to US missile-defense efforts has been to increase an already ongoing arms buildup and reaffirm the commitment to "one China" with regard to Taiwan.

India and Pakistan

India and Pakistan are relative newcomers as nuclear-weapon states and are also impacted by US missile-defense policy. Both countries surprised the world in the late 1990s with a series of nuclear tests and later entered into a brief military conflict representing one of the few times two nuclear-armed states engaged in direct military confrontation. The United States is pursuing strong ties with both India and Pakistan. President Bush recently concluded a precedent-setting agreement to share civil nuclear technology with India.[27] In addition, the United States has also offered Patriot missile-defense systems to New Delhi, which has traditionally looked to Russia for military technology.[28] The United States also values Pakistan's support in the global war on terror and is also cultivating strong relations as exemplified by President Bush's recent visit despite violent public protests and the killing of an American diplomat.[29]

India and China have an adversarial relationship due to direct competition for hegemony in South Asia. Hence, India's nuclear arsenal provides deterrence and also international prestige as a rising power in Asia. India also has tense relations with Pakistan highlighted by territorial disputes in the Kashmir region. However, India enjoys a significant military and economic advantage over Pakistan. Similar to China, India embraces minimal deterrence as the most effective nuclear strategy.[30] India's strategic policy considers nuclear weapons as primarily political tools. Therefore, India sizes its nuclear force to be a credible deterrent against China with the assumption that Pakistan's lesser threat will also be deterred.

In Pakistan, nuclear weapons and ballistic missiles are a deterrent against Indian aggression and a great source of national pride. Despite a weak economy and political difficulties, Pakistan's army invests heavily in its missile force to counter India's growing might.[31] In addition, Pakistan has forged strong ties with China and North Korea as a means to acquire nuclear and missile technology to keep pace with India. Pakistan's nuclear strategy is explicitly linked to India's nuclear arsenal declaring a policy of matching any increase in Indian nuclear forces with a corresponding increase in Pakistan.[32]

US missile-defense policy is likely to have an indirect effect on India and Pakistan. As discussed previously, US missile-defense policy could result in a further increase in Chinese ballistic missiles. Accordingly, India may increase its nuclear missile force to maintain a minimum deterrent against its primary nemesis in China. The next domino in the chain reaction is a possible Pakistani military expansion to match India's escalation. However, there are other factors that could moderate the likelihood of Indian and Pakistani increases in nuclear weapons. For example, India may not increase its forces if China only increases long-range ICBMs clearly targeted at the United States. In addition, China, India, and Pakistan are increasingly investing in mobile- or sheltered-ballistic-missile systems which will be difficult to target.[33] Consequently, the increased survivability may eliminate a perceived need for additional quantity. In any event, the existence of the US missile-defense system is not a primary issue for India and Pakistan but could lead to increased arsenals due to perturbations in regional security relationships.

North Korea, Iran, and Iraq

One of the main objectives of MDA's limited long-range ballistic-missile-defense capability was to dissuade and deter threats from countries such as members of the axis of evil: Iraq, North Korea, and Iran. The US invasion and occupation has mitigated ballistic-missile concerns in Iraq, but North Korea and Iran continue as threats. Unfortunately, the United States has adversarial relations with Iran and North Korea with repeated threats of military action from all parties. Moreover US military interventions over the past decade have justifiably heightened fears of military operations against these two countries. North Korea's Kim Chong-Il has consistently threatened to preemptively launch WMD attacks against the United States, South Korea, Japan, or any other US ally. North Korea's launch of the Taepo Dong ballistic missile over Japan is clear indication of the seriousness of the threat. Likewise, Iran's radical president has promised to "wipe Israel off the map" and has also threatened WMD attacks against the United States for interfering with Iran's internal activities.[34] Iran's threats are not to be taken lightly given its use of ballistic missiles and WMD to target Iraq's population during the "war of the cities" in the Iran-Iraq war and its current pursuit of uranium enrichment technology.[35] The decision to focus US missile-defense efforts against Iran and North Korea is justified given the acrimonious relationships.

Beyond ill will, both North Korea and Iran possess credible WMD and ballistic-missile programs. North Korea is widely assessed to already possess nuclear capability, while Iran recently announced plans to resume research in uranium enrichment. Iran claims its nuclear program is for peaceful purposes, but there is ample evidence that it aspires to possess a nuclear weapon capability. The development of an indigenous uranium-enrichment capability would open the door for Iran to produce weapons-grade uranium and plutonium. Both countries also possess domestic ballistic-missile capability. North Korea's Taepo Dong missile, in a three stage configuration, has an estimated range of 15,000 km which could hit anywhere in North America. Likewise, Iran has a large inventory of short-to-medium range ballistic missiles including the Shahab-3 which can reach Israel with its 1,300 km reach.[36] Moreover, both countries have a history of illegally proliferating ballistic missile technology thereby increasing the overall threat to the United States.[37]

North Korea continues to engage in negotiations to renounce its WMD programs in return for international support and security guarantees. The "Six Party" talks involving North Korea, South Korea, Russia, China, Japan, and the United States are making progress, but North Korea's history of irrational behavior and reneging on promises suggests caution is in order.

North Korea is uniquely vulnerable to missile defense due to its low number of missiles, geography, and failing economy. First, North Korea's limited number and relatively unsophisticated missiles create doubt that it could overwhelm or fool the existing and planned US missile-defense system. Second, geography works against North Korea as it is a small country on a peninsula. Consequently, US sea- , land- , and air-based missile-defense assets can flank the country and maximize the likelihood of intercept. Finally, North Korea has a failing economy and can not afford the arms buildup needed to guarantee defeat of the US missile-defense system.

North Korea runs the risk of imploding, much as Reagan's strategic defense initiative created uncertainty for Russia and contributed to Soviet economic collapse. There is little public evidence from North Korean officials to evaluate how significant a factor the US missile-defense program was in their decision to pursue negotiations. However, it is likely more than coincidence that North Korea agreed to more substantive disarmament discussions in the same timeframe that US missile-defense interceptors began their operational deployment. Therefore, even a limited US missile-defense program could contribute to the overall US goal of dissuading and deterring North Korea.

Iran continues to defy the West and is unlikely to be dissuaded from pursuing its WMD and ballistic-missile programs. Iranian leaders believe Iraq was vulnerable to US invasion, because it did not have nuclear weapons and long-range ballistic missiles.[38] Moreover, Iran's new, more radical leadership has cultivated strong ties with Russia and China. Indeed, Russia is building Iran's Bushehr nuclear power plant, has defended Iran's right to civilian nuclear technology, and has significantly increased arms sales including a billion-dollar sale of surface-to-air missiles announced in the midst of international efforts to stop Iran from its uranium enrichment program.[39] China has also invited Iran to be an observer in the Shanghai Cooperation Organization, which is emerging as a cohesive bloc to counter US interests in central Asia.[40] Finally, Iran's religious extremism leaves little room for negotiation with the West and particularly the United States.

Iran is not as vulnerable as North Korea to the planned US missile-defense system. First, Iran is a relatively large country, and the United States will not be able to count on basing rights or cooperation from neighboring countries given their instability and shifting allegiances. Indeed, Iran will have significant flexibility in moving its missiles to evade the limited range of the currently planned US boost-phase BMD systems much as Scuds avoided early intercepts in the first Gulf War. This will place the burden on the GMD and terminal-defense systems.

At present, the GMD system cannot intercept many important missiles trajectories from the Middle East due to the lack of a suitably located interceptor site. A third GMD interceptor site to defend against ballistic missiles from the Middle East is planned for the future. As mentioned in chapter 3, a disadvantage of terminal BMD is that the interceptors must be physically close to the defended target. Thus, the defender must have enough terminal-defense systems to protect every possible target. The United States and its allies do not have enough terminal-BMD systems to cover all of the potential targets within reach of Iran's growing missile force. Finally, Iran enjoys substantial profit from oil and can afford to increase and modernize its missile force to overwhelm and defeat the US midcourse-defense system.

Israel and Japan

Israel and Japan are the two most receptive countries to US missile-defense plans in Asia and are actively involved in joint programs. The missile threat to Israel and Japan's homeland is possibly more tangible than for even the United States. Israel in particular is surrounded by sworn enemies who have repeatedly attacked the nation through various means including ballistic missile attack. Japan is also threatened by neighbors in close geographic proximity in North Korea with China becoming more of a concern for the long term.

The history and cooperation between the United States and Israel illuminates some of the key dynamics of missile-defense systems. First, missile-defense systems have tremendous political value, but these systems can lose that value very quickly if they do not perform up to expectations. In the first Gulf War, the deployment of the Patriot TMD system was politically critical to keeping the Arab coalition together, as Israel was willing to forgo retaliation against Iraq in lieu of defense. However, it was the poor design of the Scud missile which minimized damage and not the Patriot PAC-2, which was not designed for missile defense and actually performed poorly.[41] The course of the war could have changed significantly if the Scuds had caused more damage leading to Israeli military retaliation and subsequent chaos in the US-Arab coalition.

Realizing the imperative need for improvement over the PAC-2, Israel and the United States collaborated on the Arrow missile which is an Israeli theater BMD system.[42] The Arrow started as a joint venture in 1988 with a first flight in 1990. However, a substantial upgrade, the Arrow 2, began after the Scud attacks in the 1991 Gulf War. The first Arrow 2 battery was deployed in

2000 after $1 billion in investment between the United States and Israel. Operational testing continues as highlighted by a successful December 2005 test in the United States.[43] The Arrow is expected to be fully integrated into Israel's tiered defense system by the end of the decade to include interoperability with selected US missile-defense systems.

Japan and the United States began missile-defense cooperation in 1999 after North Korea's test firing of a ballistic missile over Japan. The initial agreement focused on research and development with the level of cooperation increasing in recent years to include agreements on fielding new systems. In December 2005, the two countries confirmed plans to build a large tracking radar in Japan to support both Japanese and US missile-defense efforts.[44] The location of a high-power tracking radar in Japan will provide a substantial boost in detection and tracking capabilities for both countries. Japan's government also approved a nine-year, $1.2 billion plan to field its own Aegis BMD capability along with Patriot PAC-3 in order to form a layered defense.[45] The first missiles are scheduled to come online in 2007. In addition, Japan is cooperating with the United States on a new sea-based interceptor, improved command and control, and intelligence sharing. Japan is clearly the most significant missile-defense partner in East Asia, and the increasing level of cooperation is essential for success of the US missile-defense program.

Nonstate Actors

Nonstate actors such as al-Qaeda and the Khan Research Laboratories also impact US missile-defense policy in Asia. The likelihood of a terrorist-sponsored, long-range, ballistic-missile attack against the United States is low due to the magnitude of resources required.[46] However, terrorist groups are more than capable of acquiring and launching theater ballistic or cruise missiles against the United States, deployed forces, or allies. Events such as 9/11 and the USS *Cole* attack demonstrate that assaults of this scale are possible, and modern terrorist groups have the will to do them. Moreover countries, such as Iran, sponsor terrorists and can provide ballistic-missile systems to rogue groups willing to use them. The Rumsfeld report is often cited for predicting the North Korean long-range ballistic-missile threat; however, the report also highlighted the far more likely occurrence of short-range off-shore attacks.[47] Congress and the MDA are becoming increasingly concerned with this issue and are moving to further investigate the threat.[48]

Transnational corporations are also key players in Asia and missile defense. The rise of globalization and multinational corporations allow individuals and companies to operate beyond the reach of any single government. A. Q. Khan and his Khan Research Laboratories are now recognized as one of the most damaging conduits for nuclear proliferation in the past two decades. His clandestine efforts to acquire foreign technology enabled Pakistan's surprising entry into the nuclear club in 1998 by stealing and buying technology.[49] In 2001 Khan was arrested after he was discovered to have masterminded an international nuclear-proliferation ring that included customers in Iran, Libya, and North Korea.[50] Moreover, Khan later confessed that his network operated worldwide with operatives in nations as diverse as Dubai, China, and Germany with numerous middlemen and suppliers.[51] Hence, the modern era of globalization and technology sharing permits individuals and private groups to also impact issues, such as WMD and missile defense, which were formerly the exclusive domain of nation-states.

Intelligence, awareness, and flexibility are keys to defending against a potential terrorist ballistic-missile attack; and these characteristics should also drive missile-defense requirements. Global and persistent intelligence, surveillance, and reconnaissance are required since there will be little intentional warning; and attacks can come from a wide range of locations and methods. Consequently, the US missile-defense system must have a global network of sensors and intelligence-gathering agencies feeding an efficient command-and-control system.

Furthermore, a flexible, layered defense is essential to providing multiple engagement opportunities against a surprise attack. Indeed, theater-defense systems will likely play a great role in deterring and defeating terrorist ballistic-missile attacks due to the need for mobility and flexible employment. While the interceptors get much of the attention, the unique aspects of terrorist attacks and transnational-technology proliferation in

Asia also drive the need for a robust, global intelligence network and highly integrated command-and-control system.

Conclusion

Asia's complex political and strategic environment will strongly influence the success or failure of the current US missile-defense program. Unlike the Cold War where US strategic policy was centered on a single, well-understood country, the new Asian landscape hosts multiple and competing alliances with several nations vying for regional hegemony. No other continent promises as many challenges after the breakup of the Soviet Union, the rise of Asian economic power, the spread of Islamic fundamentalism, and the process of globalization. Hence, the United States must find a coherent missile-defense policy that will best handle the range of actors from emerging transnational terrorists to new nuclear states to tried and true Cold War adversaries.

The current US policy of limited missile defense and engaging international partners is the best course of action. The United States does not have the technical means or the funding to field a credible missile defense against Russia's nuclear ICBM force. In addition, China is already substantially improving the quality of its nuclear force and, with time, could also overwhelm the US missile defense against long-range ballistic missiles. A significant increase in China's arsenal could ripple through Asia inducing destabilizing force-level escalation in India, Pakistan, and Japan. However, this could happen even without the existence of missile-defense systems. For example, US and Soviet missile inventories increased in the 1970s and 1980s *after* the signing of the 1972 ABM Treaty.

Conversely, eliminating the missile-defense system leaves US territory, deployed forces, and allies vulnerable to attack which will not be deterred by offensive nuclear forces alone. Ballistic-missile-attack is a reality and no longer an academic exercise. Deployed US forces, Afghanistan, Israel, Iran, Iraq, and Saudi Arabia have all been recipients of ballistic-missile attacks. Moreover, the widespread proliferation of Soviet-era missiles and technology increase the likelihood for attacks in the future. Rogue nations and terrorists are far less likely to be deterred by nuclear retaliation as the United States and the Soviet Union were during the Cold War. As a result, ballistic-missile-defense becomes imperative for US interests in Asia.

Notes

1. Cirincione, "Declining Ballistic Missile Threat," 2–4.
2. MIT, Lincoln Laboratory, seminar.
3. Miller and Trenin, *Russian Military*, 27–28.
4. Cohen, *Failed Crusade*, 98–106.
5. Miller and Trenin, *Russian Military*, 7–8.
6. Schneider, *Nuclear Forces*, 10.
7. Ivanov, "Russia Must Be Strong."
8. Schneider, *Nuclear Forces*, 10–12.
9. Goldgeier and McFaul, "What To Do About Russia, 46.
10. Sieff, "BMD Focus."
11. Allison, *Nuclear Terrorism*, 15.
12. "Megatons to Megawatts."
13. Edwards and Kemp, *Russia's Wrong Direction*, 5.
14. Farah, "Russia Equips Iran."
15. Wirtz and Larsen, *Rockets' Red Glare*, 187.
16. Ibid.
17. Morgan, "China's economy."
18. Ibid.
19. *Annual Report to Congress.*
20. Martin, "Theater Ballistic Missiles," 5.
21. "China says US weapons."
22. Krepon, *Cooperative Threat Reduction*, 138–39.
23. FAS, *Unclassified Summary of a National Intelligence Estimate.*
24. Krepon, *Cooperative Threat Reduction*, 142.
25. Wirtz and Larsen, *Rockets' Red Glare*, 184.
26. Oster, "China Plans 15% Boost."
27. "Bush, India's Singh Sign."
28. Hali, "Should Pakistan Panic?" 1.
29. Hunt, "Bush Celebrates India Nuclear Deal."
30. Wirtz and Larsen, *Rockets' Red Glare*, 244.
31. Krepon, *Cooperative Threat Reduction*, 153.
32. Ibid., 150.
33. FAS, *Unclassified Summary.*
34. "Iranian's 'Wipe Israel Off Map.'"
35. Ali, "Chemical Weapons," 43.
36. FAS, *Unclassified Summary.*
37. Langewiesche, "Wrath of Khan," Part II, 62–85.
38. Nuclear Threat Institute, *WMD411: Your Information Resource.*
39. Meyer, "Russian Defense Minister."
40. "Iran, China Study."

41. Conyers, "Opening Statement."
42. Miller, "Israel's Arrow Defense."
43. Katz, "Arrow Can now Intercept."
44. Igarashi, "US to Deploy Radar."
45. Roosevelt, "MDA Moves Forward."
46. Krepon, *Cooperative Threat Reduction*, 4.
47. FAS, *Executive Summary*.
48. "Obering: Decision."
49. Langewiesche, "Wrath of Khan," Part I, 63.
50. Ibid., 64.
51. *GlobalSecurity.org*, "Weapons of Mass Destruction."

Chapter 5

Conclusions

*I believe that it is strategically and morally necessary to build
a missile defense. Strategically, because of the proliferation
of weapons of mass destruction and the missile technology
to deliver them. Morally, because the doctrine of mutual
assured destruction, which I have opposed in my writings for
at least thirty years, is bankrupt. It may have had a limited
theoretical sense in a two-power nuclear world, but in a multi-
nuclear world, it is reckless.*

—Henry Kissinger
Testimony to Congress, 1999

The US missile-defense program is an essential element for
assuring allies and successfully dissuading, deterring, and defeating asymmetric threats to US interests worldwide and especially in Asia. US missile-defense policy was buffeted by international and domestic politics during the Cold War leading to a
lack of consensus on the utility, cost, and technical capability.
Consequently, missile defense was marginalized and yielded to
the strategic doctrine of MAD. However, the post–Cold War world
is quite different, and strategies which worked in a bipolar
world of peer competitors are no longer sufficient to handle the
broad range of threats now in existence. Nowhere is this phe-
nomenon more apparent than in Asia where the breakup of the
Soviet Union, proliferation of WMD, rise of Islamic fundamentalism, and emerging regional powers collude to create an exceed-
ingly complex strategic environment. Furthermore, this complex
new environment requires a new and more balanced approach
to strategic thinking which incorporates strategic defense.

The United States documented the changing global environment in 2001 by designating a new triad of strategic capabilities including nuclear and conventional offensive forces, strategic defenses, and responsive infrastructure. Strategic defenses
are now essential because many adversaries, such as terrorists
or rogue nations, are not deterred by threats of nuclear retaliation. These adversaries are committed to asymmetric warfare

against the United States, and ballistic missiles and WMD are ideal weapons, as they allow a less-capable adversary to threaten the United States by striking at a perceived weakness. Since the 1972 ABM Treaty, the United States intentionally allowed itself to be vulnerable to Soviet ballistic-missile attack as part of MAD doctrine. However, many adversaries now possess ballistic missiles, have used them in the past, and will almost certainly use them in the future against the United States, deployed forces, and allies. Thus, intentionally remaining vulnerable to ballistic-missile attack is no longer a prudent policy, and the United States is committed to fielding a BMD system.

The MDA is tasked with developing the US missile-defense system and is pursuing a limited-layered-defense capability. The system is limited in that it is only designed to stop a small number of missiles, and no pretence is made toward being able to stop a large-scale attack. The system is layered in that elements are designed to engage missiles in boost, midcourse, and terminal phases allowing the best opportunity for successful intercepts. Thus, the current missile defense seeks to strike a balance between not recklessly threatening the value of traditional strategic deterrence while maximizing deterrent and operational effectiveness against lower-tier adversaries.

Substantial controversy remains on the cost and technical feasibility of missile defense. The United States has spent over $100 billion on missile defense since 1983, and the first elements of a nascent operational capability are just now within grasp. Moreover, key elements of the missile-defense system, such as the GMD, have mixed test results and have not consistently proven themselves in realistic scenarios. The baseline boost-phase system, the ABL, is years behind schedule with costs already triple the initial $1.5 billion estimate.[1] Moreover, the ABL has significant operational issues such as limited persistence, short lethal range, and basing requirements. The MDA programs that have a longer developmental legacy, such as Patriot and the Aegis BMD, show the most consistency and promise for operational utility. However, even these systems are plagued by skeptics who question their true effectiveness such as the controversy over Patriot performance in Iraq. Hence, the technical immaturity, lack of realistic testing, and questionable operational effectiveness of the MDA's missile-defense portfolio creates substantial doubt as to whether these systems will do the job.

Beyond technology issues, Asia's complex political and strategic environment also complicate missile-defense policy. Just as in the Cold War, Russia remains the only country capable of destroying the United States with its large nuclear arsenal. Therefore, Russian foreign policy must be a key consideration. Russia is not enamored with US plans to deploy missile defense, as this directly threatens its nuclear deterrence which is the foundation of Russian national security and a cornerstone of Russia's struggle to retain world-power status.[2] In response to US missile-defense plans, Russia is developing new maneuvering ICBMs specifically designed to defeat US missile-defense systems and has withdrawn from the START II Treaty following US abrogation of the ABM Treaty. Russian cooperation in non- and counterproliferation programs such as the Nunn-Lugar Cooperative Threat Reduction Program has cooled as well. Indeed, Russia is generally threatened by US missile-defense plans and is increasingly charting an independent course for its national security.

In addition to Russia, the emerging nuclear powers of Asia are also impacted by US missile-defense plans. US plans may have the most impact on China, which is estimated to have only 20 ICBMs capable of reaching the United States, although this number is expected to increase regardless of US missile-defense policy.[3] Even a limited US missile-defense system could impact China's perception of its nuclear deterrence and cause an escalation in the number of Chinese ICBMs. Similarly, India and Pakistan are drawn into the mix as multiple competing alliances create uncertainties and possibly destabilize the region as India seeks to match any Chinese missile increase with a corresponding expansion. Iran's WMD and ballistic-missile aspirations also drive a need for missile defense, as this country supports terrorism, has used ballistic missiles against Iraq's civilian population, and is openly threatening to attack the United States and Israel. The political utility of missile defense is also apparent by its value in negotiations, such as with North Korea, and in alliance building with Israel and Japan. Clearly, the strategic and military implications and imperatives of missile-defense systems in Asia must inform US decisions on missile-defense policy.

Recommendations

The analysis of the history of missile defense, the planned US missile-defense system, and the Asian strategic environment highlight specific recommendations. These recommendations are grouped under the following areas:

1. Technology and politics mandate a limited missile defense.

2. Ensure we have the right threat.

3. Theater missile defense is more important in the short term.

4. Assure flexibility and versatility.

5. Improve the credibility of the GMD system.

6. Go slow on unproven technology, especially space systems.

7. Foster international partnerships and engagement.

Continue to Pursue Limited Missile Defense and Field It Quickly

The foundational US strategy and policy documents call for a limited missile-defense system, and this is the right choice considering political, strategic, and technical limitations. Strategically, it is no longer advantageous for the United States to remain intentionally vulnerable to ballistic-missile attack. The United States and its allies have already suffered ballistic-missile attacks, and the proliferation of WMD and missile technology portends an even more dangerous ballistic-missile threat in the future. Moreover, many new adversaries embrace asymmetric attacks against the United States and will not be deterred by threats of massive nuclear retaliation. The imperative for genuine investment in missile defense is highlighted by the fact that virtually every nuclear-weapons-capable state is investing heavily in missile-defense systems and technology. Moreover, missile-defense systems, such as the US Patriot and Russian

S-300, are hot items on the global arms market and are actively marketed by both countries.

The likelihood of a long-range missile attack against the US mainland is low; however, the impact is tremendously high. The terrorist attacks on 9/11 were tragic, but even one nuclear weapon landing on a large US city would be at least as traumatic and more likely far worse. There is no guarantee that spending a few billion more dollars on levees would have prevented the flooding of New Orleans after Hurricane Katrina, but there is little doubt now that it would have been wise to at least try reasonable measures to avoid the estimated $50 billion in damages, plus human anguish, for which there is no dollar value equivalent.

Current technical and political realities obviate pursuit of an "unlimited," all-encompassing missile shield. The best architectures for defense against large-scale missile attack would require hundreds to thousands of space-based interceptors.[4] Study after study has concluded that this approach is unaffordable, well beyond the state of technology, and would grossly exceed the United States' ability to launch and maintain such an enormous satellite constellation.[5]

Even if the tremendous technical challenges could be overcome, political issues would also preclude an absolute missile defense. First, a comprehensive missile shield would threaten Russian and Chinese security and could lead to a destabilizing and pointless arms race. Both of these countries have the resources to build effective countermeasures and asymmetric tactics faster and more cheaply than the United States could upgrade a comprehensive missile-defense system. Furthermore, the legacy and impact of US domestic politics also reduces the ability of the United States to field more than a limited missile defense in a timely manner. The divisive nature of missile-defense discourse historically leads to compromise as exemplified throughout the Cold War and 1990s. A sufficient political consensus is not achievable to support the decades of research and development, and the additional hundreds of billions of dollars needed to attempt a comprehensive missile-defense system. It is far more preferable to field a limited defense in a timely fashion and mature the technologies needed for space.

Make Sure We Have the Right Threat

The United States should conduct a broader review of WMD and the missile threat to ensure we are tackling the right problems. The MDA is currently chartered to develop systems to defend against ballistic missiles. However, the current focus on defending against surface-to-surface ballistic missiles represents straight-line conventional thinking and excludes many asymmetric missile threats that may be more likely to occur and even more dangerous. Much of the rhetoric on missile defense is still focused on yesterday's well-understood ICBM threat, but does not give sufficient voice to new or unconventional missile or WMD threats as described in the most recent *Quadrennial Defense Review.*[6]

For example, the current missile-defense system has little capability against cruise missiles. Cruise missiles are far easier to obtain than long-range ballistic missiles, as there are 130 cruise-missile types distributed among 75 nations.[7] The cruise missile is often called the "poor man's air force" and can conceivably be launched against US interests from small vessels off shore.[8] Moreover, Scuds and cruise missiles can be purchased for $100K on the open market and will fit in a small vessel or standard shipping container.[9] At present, very few shipping containers are physically inspected due to the immense volume of containers and the limited number of inspectors.[10] As Adm Thomas Keating, the commander of United States Northern Command (NORTHCOM) stated: "We have a very limited capability to deter a cruise missile attack. Someone can pull the tarp off a 110-foot tramp steamer off the coast of Boston and shoots [sic] an unguided cruise missile into Boston. Can't do much about it, we want to get better at that."[11] The FY 2006 Appropriations Report amplifies this concern as Congress provided $10 million for the MDA to investigate "the possibility of an asymmetric missile threat against the United States homeland where terrorists would move short-range missiles closer to the United States on sea-based platforms."[12]

Furthermore, Russia, China, and Iran have publicly announced strategies to use unconventional long-range missile attack to stun the United States. Russian and Chinese threats are well-documented and include planned uses of decoys and countermeasures.[13] Even Iran's missile testing indicates it is developing the capability for exploding a nuclear weapon high above the United States to produce an electromagnetic pulse attack.[14] An EMP attack could cripple electronic systems throughout the United States. This type of attack may not kill many directly, but it could dramatically affect all Americans as our power, financial, and communications systems are disrupted or destroyed.[15] The current missile-defense system will have limited capability to deal with this threat for several years, as there is no boost-phase system able to intercept the missile early, and we have not even selected a GMD site to defend against threats from the Middle East. More importantly, there is no *requirement* driving the current system to cover this threat.

The MDA is responsible for defining the threat its systems will defeat, and this system may need to be changed. This arrangement has the acquisition benefit of allowing stable requirements, but these stable requirements may not be the right requirements. Congress and the MDA are beginning to look at additional threats, such as cruise missile and off-shore launches, but the pace of threat definition needs to accelerate to ensure that the right systems and tactics are developed. This may require organizations other than the MDA, such as United States Strategic Command and/or NORTHCOM take the lead or at least have greater input into threat definition and requirements. Clearly, stable requirements assist acquisition in building the system right, but more effort and better organization is needed to ensure we build the right systems.

Theater Missile Defense Is More Important in the Near Term

The United States should maintain priority on ensuring that short- and medium-range missile-defense systems are rigorously tested, rapidly deployed, and continuously upgraded. The presidential policy directive *NSPD-23* eliminated the distinction between national and theater missile defense; however, one of the consequences of this action was to obscure the importance of theater missile defenses from the national debate.[16] The threat of ocean spanning North Korean or Chinese missiles landing on Los Angeles grabs the headlines and stirs popular emotion, but short- and medium-range ballistic missiles are far more available, deployed, and used than their ICBM brethren.

The global ICBM threat is actually declining while the threat from short- and medium-range ballistic missiles is increasing in diversity and lethality. From 1987 to 2005, the number of ICBMs (including SLBMs) dropped 51 percent from just over 4,000 to under 2,000.[17] This number is expected to drop even more as the United States and Russia continue to draw down in accordance with the 2002 Strategic Offensive Reductions Treaty. Furthermore, deployed IRBMs plummeted 97 percent from 1987 to 2005 with China's 20 DF-4 missiles the only remaining inventory. Outside of the five NPT nuclear states, only Iran and North Korea are considered possible candidates to field IRBMs/ICBMs over the next decade, and the likelihood of an ICBM attack against the US mainland is deemed unlikely.[18]

Conversely, the proliferation of medium- and short-range ballistic missiles is increasing. Since the late 1980s, India, Iran, North Korea, Pakistan, and Saudi Arabia have fielded their first MRBM.[19] This represents the most significant increase in the diversity of the ballistic missile threat and is focused in Asia. Taiwan's Ministry of Defense also announced China has accelerated its buildup of theater ballistic missiles and will have 1,800 TBMs poised for launch across the Taiwan Strait by 2010.[20] Moreover, over 30 nations possess SRBM and countries such as Russia, China, North Korea, Syria, and Pakistan continue to export systems and technology.[21] In reference to MRBMs and SRBMs, the 2001 CIA estimate on the ballistic-missile threat predicts: "Emerging ballistic missile states continue to increase the range, reliability, and accuracy of the [short- and medium-range] missile systems in their inventories—posing ever greater risk to US forces, interests, and allies throughout the world."[22] Moreover, the commander of American forces in Korea announced Pyongyang recently tested an advanced, solid-fuel short-range missile and that "North Korea in recent years had been focusing its missile program on developing short-range missiles that could be used in a conflict on the Korean peninsula."[23] Thus, short- to medium-range ballistic missiles in Asia represent a greater near-term threat to US interests than intermediate- or long-range missiles.

A flexible and effective defense against MRBMs and SRBMs is the most salient issue for every Asian state or nonstate actor analyzed in chapter 4, with the possible exception of Russia. However, even Russia is a major factor as it widely exports TBMs and ABM systems throughout Asia. Furthermore, the use of TBMs is now an accepted international norm after decades of repeated use by many nations.[24] TBMs are now well integrated into operational military strategy such as China's plan for defending the Straights of Taiwan. Clearly, the United States should increase efforts to ensure systems, such as the Aegis BMD, Patriot, and THAAD, are well-funded and do not get overshadowed or delayed by more controversial systems such as the GMD or ABL.

Furthermore, the United States should prioritize evolutionary development of theater systems over leap-ahead technology when possible. For example, the ABL is the baseline BPI system, but it will not be available for operational deployment for many years. A better solution is to anoint a sea- or land-based alternative as the baseline system and increase funding for a high-speed interceptor suitable to the boost-phase mission. This solution could increase theater missile-defense capability and is more likely to provide the United States with a credible near-term boost-phase capability.

The Aegis BMD has demonstrated substantial ability to track and engage midcourse- and terminal-phase targets. Moreover, Japan and the United States are already collaborating on a high-speed interceptor upgrade for the Aegis BMD. As evidence of the near-term benefit of a high-speed interceptor, a Japanese official stated a single Aegis BMD cruiser with a new high-speed missile could defend the entire Japanese mainland as opposed to four ships equipped with the current SM-3 missile.[25] An Aegis-based high-speed interceptor not only delivers a faster path to operational utility, but it also provides an avenue to field the desperately needed multiple kill vehicle as that technology matures.

Thus, an increased emphasis on promising "theater" ballistic missile defenses could provide near-term operational benefit and a more manageable path to new capabilities such as multiple kill and boost-phase intercept. This approach is more affordable and achievable than banking solely on unpredictable leap-ahead technology which takes decades to develop and provides little interim capability.

Finally, the United States needs to expand its missile-defense focus from research and development to include supporting global operation of TMD systems. Under the capabilities-based acquisition construct, the MDA was wisely given license to pursue incremental block upgrades in order to expedite fielding new capability. However, some of these systems are now online and it is imperative that the MDA develop an effective combat-support function to ensure the TMD systems are integrated into a global missile-defense command-and-control structure. This will be a difficult challenge as the MDA, US Strategic Command, and the services attempt to balance competing requirements, limited resources, and complex command relationships. This challenge must be overcome as the TMD systems are guaranteed to be needed in combat, and these systems must work.

Emphasize Flexible and Versatile Systems

Flexibility and versatility are tenets of air and space power and are also highly desirable attributes for the missile-defense system. Many missile-defense elements will only perform their ABM mission a small fraction of the time. Therefore, these systems need to enhance their value by seamlessly handling other critically important missions. The ability to perform other missions and impact decision makers at the tactical, operational, and strategic levels increases the military value and thereby constituency of supporters for missile-defense systems.

For example, the Aegis BMD, Patriot, and THAAD systems can support air defense as well as missile defense. Consequently, these systems will always have advocates in the services who value their ability to protect fielded forces from aircraft. In addition, these systems are mobile allowing flexible operation around the world which is particularly true of the Aegis system that can effectively perform a host of functions with its long range, sea-based, advanced communications, radar, and variety of armaments. The early-warning-radars and command-and-control systems are also tremendously versa-

MDA Photo

Sea-based X-band radar can simultaneously support missile defense and space surveillance

tile, as they can track an inbound missile for destruction while also serving vital national-intelligence and space-control needs by providing 24/7 space situational awareness.

Conversely, high-cost ABM systems such as the ABL and GMD need to explore secondary missions and better define their value when not engaging threat missiles. Much as the F-22 fighter needed to add a ground-attack role to placate critics, the ABL needs to demonstrate important functions that it can perform in the vast majority of time that it is not engaged in missile defense. Otherwise, these systems will not prove attractive to joint commanders or national decision makers who will likely see them as a funding source for other more near-term needs. Without an enduring base of support and military value, single-mission systems are likely to fall victim to partisan politics or budget reductions much as the Nike-Zeus, Sentinel, Spartan, Brilliant Pebbles, GPALs, and NMD systems of the past.

Improve Technical Credibility and Performance of GMD System

The technical credibility and performance of the GMD system must improve to maximize its deterrent and defense effectiveness. The inconsistent record of performance of the GMD system diminishes confidence that it will be able to effectively intercept even a limited ICBM attack. Several internal and independent reviews of the GMD system acknowledge this fact and recommend increased focus on quality control, testing, and systems engineering.[26] Indeed, Congress redirected $150 million in FY 2006 for the GMD program to emphasize these areas.[27] The sensor and command-and-control elements have performed more consistently; however, the United States must maintain the emphasis on networking the far-flung array of sensors, interceptors, communication links, and battle management to produce a system that will work efficiently in the no-notice, short-timeline world of ballistic-missile defense.

Another needed improvement is to quickly field a third interceptor site to cover missile threats from countries like Iran in central and southwest Asia. Chapter 4's assessment of the Asian environment shows that several countries in this region possess the capability and malicious intent to attack US interests. However, the current GMD system has no capability to intercept missiles on westward trajectories from Asia. The MDA is currently evaluating locations in Poland and elsewhere in Europe for a third site.[28] Clearly, political factors will impact the location and development of the site, but the fact remains that the GMD system will have little deterrent or defensive utility against Iran until the third site is operational.

Beyond improving the readiness of the baseline-operational system, the MDA must also maintain a focused-development program to overcome limitations in target discrimination and interceptor performance. To the MDA's credit, the current baseline system is not advertised to have capability against countermeasures. However, it is widely believed that any actor capable of acquiring an ICBM is also likely capable of fielding a wide range of, simple but effective, countermeasures.[29] Consequently, the MDA must continue to place high priority on technologies and tactics to increase the probability of kill against targets employing even simple techniques. For example, promising efforts, such as the multiple-kill-vehicle program, enhanced IR seekers with multicolor-focal planes and increased resolution, and improved discrimination algorithms must remain high priority. In addition, a reliable, high-speed, and more maneuverable booster would be greatly beneficial and should be given high priority in order to improve GMD performance.

Go slow on Unproven Technology, Increase Testing, and be Wary of Rushing to Space

The missile-defense program must go slow on high-risk unproven technology. One of the favorite (and most effective) arguments of missile-defense critics is that over $100 billion has been spent with little return on investment. Technical overreach is one of the key contributors to this malady. Much like national-security space systems, missile defense depends upon layers of incredibly complex cutting-edge technology and networks that must work perfectly in order to achieve success. Failure of even a single component, software program, human operator, or acts of God can easily cause disaster. Complex-systems theorists have proven repeatedly that sophisticated systems like the missile-defense network are difficult to accurately model and have unpredictable behavior.[30] Therefore, the complexity of missile-defense systems demands increased emphasis on systems engineering and extensive testing in operationally relevant environments—modeling and analysis is not good enough.

Indeed, in the rush to sell new programs or keep existing ones alive, government and industry officials accept risky and unproven technology that looks good on PowerPoint briefings but is not ready for field use. Thus, it is no surprise that missile-defense systems are plagued by huge cost overruns, schedule delays, and performance failures. Consequently, much like the current overhaul in space-systems acquisition, missile defense must also reduce technical risk through increased testing, reduced reliance on unproven technology, and terminating under-performing programs to increase focus and free up resources.[31]

The Space Tracking and Surveillance System (STSS) and ABL are examples of programs that demonstrate the effects of prematurely base-lining high-risk technology and not hitting the brakes fast enough. The STSS is the current incarnation of the previous Space and Missile Tracking System and space-based infrared sensor (SBIRS) low. In 2001 the GAO declared five of six critical SBIRS low technologies were immature more than five years *after* the acquisition start date. After nearly a decade of development and billions of dollars in overruns, the STSS was finally reduced to a demonstration of two satellites. A decision to develop an operational satellite will now wisely wait until after the demonstration in space.[32]

The ABL is suffering the same unrealistic expectations that hampered the STSS, as it is designated the nation's primary boost-phase missile-defense element but has not even demonstrated all of the key technologies in a relevant environment. The first airborne live-fire event is not scheduled until 2008, which is more than three years later than originally scheduled.[33] Much like the STSS, the ABL requires several advancements to the state-of-the-art and is unlikely to be ready for primetime use for many years. The MDA is making a wise move to slow down the ABL program and take more time to develop the technology.[34] Even more encouraging is the decision to delay purchase of the second aircraft until after the lethal shoot-down demonstration.[35] Furthermore, instead of trying to solve all of the miracles on one program with artificial need dates, the development burden could be spread to other ABL programs such as the current Air Force effort to mount a laser in a C-130.[36] The MDA can focus on the hardest problems for missile defense while leveraging lessons learned from other efforts.

More tough decisions like the ABL downgrade are needed earlier in the development cycle to reinforce a "fly-before-buy" strategy, especially for space systems. Many missile-defense advocates pine for rapidly fielding space-based interceptors and exotic sensors. However, the Brilliant Pebbles, the STSS, the ABL, the SBIRS high, the National Polar-orbiting Operational Environmental Satellite System (NPOESS), the advanced extremely high frequency (EHF), the wideband gap filler, the evolved expendable launch vehicle (EELV), the space radar, and the transformational satellite (TSAT) experiences should temper enthusiasm for racing to space as these complex systems are costly, challenging, and risky as shown in table 2.

Virtually every major space acquisition is severely over budget and years behind schedule largely due to adopting immature technology, unrealistic requirements, and optimistic schedules.[37] Even with additional time and funding, many of these concepts may not reach the field due to unforeseen technical limitations

Table 2. Current space acquisition difficulties

Space Program	Function	Status
NPOESS	Weather Observation	$3 billion overrun and at least 17 months late[a]
SBIRS High	Missile Launch Early Warning	$6 billion overrun (150%), six years late, technical issues[b]
SBIRS Low (now STSS technical demonstration)	Missile Launch Early Warning	Cancelled due to immature technology, cost escalated from $10 billion to over $23 billion, years behind schedule[c]
ABL	Missile Defense	Downgraded to technical demonstration; 350% overrun, years late[d]
EELV	Satellite Launch	>$14 billion overrun, years late[e]
Space Radar	ISR	Congress continues to cut funding citing immature technology and high cost[f]
TSAT	Communications	Congress continues to cut funding citing immature technology and high cost[g]
Advanced EHF	Communications	> $1billion overrun, 50% unit cost growth, years late[h]
Wideband Gap Filler	Communications	Increasing cost, >two years late on "low risk" satellite[i]

[a]Congressman Sherwood Boehlert (R-NY), *Opening Statement on NPOESS IG* [inspector general] *Report Hearing*, US House of Representatives, House Science and Technology Committee, Washington DC, 11 May 2006, http://gop.science.house.gov/hearings/full06/May%2011/sbopening.pdf.
[b]Marcia Smith, *Military Space Programs: Issues Concerning DoD's SBIRS and STSS Programs*, Congressional Research Service, RS21148, 25 November 2005, http://www.cnie.org/NLE/CRSreports/06feb/RS21148.pdf.
[c]Ibid.
[d]*Defense Acquisitions: Status of Ballistic Missile Defense Program in 2004*, United States Government Accountability Office Report to Congressional Committees, March 2005, http://www.gao.gov/new.items/d05243.pdf.
[e]Raymond Decker, *Defense Space Activities: Continuation of Evolved Expendable Launch Vehicle Program's Progress to Date Subject to Some Uncertainty*, United States General Accounting Office Report to Congressional Committees, 24 June 2004, http://www.gao.gov/htext/d03379.html.
[f]Marcia Smith, *Military Space Programs: Issues Concerning DoD's SBIRS and STSS Programs*, Congressional Research Service, RS21148, 25 November 2005, http://www.cnie.org/NLE/CRSreports/06feb/RS21148.pdf.
[g]Ibid.
[h]Ibid.
[i]Ibid.

or political realities. Consequently, MDA must avoid attempting to field immature technology, terminate concepts which do not prove themselves in testing, and reward the efforts that get the job done.

Continue Partnerships and Engagement

The United States should continue to pursue international partnerships and engagement on missile defense. As demonstrated in chapter 4, missile defense is a critical national-security issue throughout Asia and also for much of the rest of the world. As a result, allies are looking to the United States for support and security guarantees in the face of rapid proliferation of ballistic missiles. Moreover, the United States also needs partners for basing rights and to assist in protecting widely dispersed interests and deployed forces. The location of interceptor sites, such as the proposed European locale for GMD, gets much of the attention; but partnerships are also vital for sensor basing such as the large radars in England, Greenland, and Japan (future). The global war on terror illustrated the value of intelligence sharing among international partners, and likewise, US missile defense will also benefit from genuine information sharing from friends and allies.

Engaging Asian nations on missile defense is important to maintaining stability and enabling cooperation in other arenas. For world powers, missile defense taps into the same body of psychological- and strategic-deterrence thinking as nuclear weapons. Consequently, the heightened strategic-security implications will increase the complexity of partnering with aspiring hegemons such as Russia and China. Missile defense is not the driving factor in US relations with Russia or China, but it does play a meaningful role in the maintenance of stability and should not be ignored. In addition to stability, Russia, China, and most other nations also have a substantial interest in minimizing the threat of terrorism and proliferation of WMD. The international partnerships formed to fight terrorism, counterproliferation, and deal with rogue nations, such as North Korea and Iran, are extremely beneficial to US security. Continuous engagement on missile defense provides transparency to Asian powers and reduces the risk of misunderstanding or otherwise adversely impacting similarly critical areas of cooperation.

Future Research

There are several additional directions for further research on US missile-defense policy and development. First, a national policy for cruise missile defense is a high-priority endeavor that needs attention. Similar to the German combination of V-1 and V-2 ballistic missiles and cruise missiles, today's threat is more than simply ballistic missiles. Secondly, other topics for investigation are the key conditions and indicators for pursuing space-based interceptors. The United States has no concrete plans to use space-based interceptors for missile defense, but this may be necessary in the future. Thirdly, defining the upper bound for the limited missile defense is an interesting topic. The current plan attempts to walk the middle ground between no capability and a full defensive shield. What is the upper limit for the number of GMD interceptors and sites before this situation becomes untenable? A final idea is an investigation of the feasibility and implications of conventional and/or nuclear preemptive strike as a missile-defense policy. In reality, many missile-attack scenarios will be difficult to defeat with a system that can only respond after a launch is initiated. A preemptive strike may be the only realistic means of defending against such threats.

Concluding Remarks

The world is transitioning away from the Cold War paradigm of intentional great power vulnerability (MAD) to an era of asymmetric threats that requires a mixture of strategic offense and defense. Furthermore, the focus of the world stage is increasingly in Asia as nations and cultures emerge from the rubble of the Soviet Union, and numerous world powers contend for regional control. President Reagan suggested that technology has now reached a level of sophistication where it is reasonable to begin the missile-defense journey, and he was correct. US missile-defense policy must find firm footing to avoid the pitfalls of technical overreach and ill-advised deterioration in global relationships to genuinely protect US forces, population, and allies from ballistic-missile attack. The current US missile-defense policy is a step in the right direction, but there is extremely hard work ahead for diplomats, technologists, and warriors.

Notes

1. *Defense Acquisitions.*
2. Schneider, *Nuclear Forces*, 10.
3. Wirtz and Larsen, *Rockets' Red Glare*, 186–88.
4. Baucom, "Rise and Fall," 143–50.
5. American Physical Society (APS), *Report of the APS.*
6. Rumsfeld, *Quadrennial Defense Review.*
7. Feickert, "Missile Survey."
8. Ibid.
9. Kyl, "Unready for this Attack"; and Sieff, "BMD Watch."
10. Flynn, "America the Vulnerable," 60–61.
11. "Obering: Decision Forthcoming."
12. "Appropriators Call for Study."
13. FAS, *Unclassified Summary.*
14. Kyl, "Unready for this Attack."
15. Foster et al., *Report of the Commission to Assess.*
16. FAS, *National Security.*
17. Cirincione, "Declining Ballistic Missile Threat," 5.
18. FAS, *Unclassified Summary.*
19. Cirincione, "Declining Ballistic Missile Threat," 6.
20. Martin, "Theater Ballistic Missiles," 5.
21. Feickert, "Missile Survey."
22. FAS, *Unclassified Summary.*
23. Onishi, "US Confirms Test."
24. Feickert, "Missile Survey."
25. Roosevelt, "MDA Moves Forward."
26. Center for Defense Information (CDI), *Independent Review Team.*
27. "MDA Director Outlines Allocation."
28. Burns, "Washington Talking to Warsaw."
29. FAS, *Unclassified Summary.*
30. "Perspectives on Complex-System Engineering," 1–4.
31. Hodge, "Sega Promises;" Pasztor, "U.S.'s Lofty Plans."
32. Smith, *Military Space Programs.*
33. *Defense Acquisitions.*
34. "Troubled Airborne Laser Program."
35. CDI, *Missile Defense Agency Fiscal Year 2007.*
36. "Boeing Receives Aircraft."
37. Levin, "Space Acquisitions," 7–10.

Acronyms

ABL	airborne laser
ABM	antiballistic missile
BMD	ballistic missile defense
BMDO	Ballistic Missile Defense Organization
BPI	boost-phase intercept
BUR	"Bottom Up Review"
CTR	cooperative threat reduction
DOD	Department of Defense
DSP	Defense Support Program
EELV	evolved expendable launch vehicle
EHF	extremely high frequency
EKV	exoatmoshperic kill vehicle
EMP	electromagnetic pulse
GBI	ground-based interceptor
GMD	ground-based midcourse defense
GPALS	global protection against limited strikes
ICBM	intercontinental ballistic missile
IR	infrared
IRBM	intermediate-range ballistic missiles
KEI	kinetic-energy interceptor
LDO	limited defensive operations
MAD	mutually assured destruction
MDA	Missile Defense Agency
MRBM	medium-range ballistic missile
MKV	multiple-kill vehicle
NMD	national missile defense
NORTHCOM	United States Northern Command
NPOESS	National Polar-orbiting Operational Environmental Satellite System
NPR	*Nuclear Posture Review*
NPT	Non-Proliferation Treaty
NSPD	*National Security Presidential Directive*
OIF	Operation Iraqi Freedom
PAC	Patriot advanced capabilities
SALT	Strategic Arms Limitation Talks
SBIRS	space-based infrared sensor
SDI	Strategic Defense Initiative
SLBM	submarine-launched ballistic missile

ACRONYMS

SRBM	short-range ballistic missile
START	Strategic Arms Reduction Treaty
STSS	Space Tracking and Surveillance System
TBM	theater ballistic missile
THAAD	terminal high altitude air defense
WMD	weapon of mass destruction

Bibliography

"Aegis Tracks Separating Ballistic Missile Target." *C4I News*. 13 October 2005. http://proquest.com/.

Ali, Javed. "Chemical Weapons and the Iran-Iraq War: A Case Study in Noncompliance." *Nonproliferation Review* 8, no. 1 (Spring 2001), 43–58.

Allison, Graham. *Nuclear Terrorism: The Ultimate Preventable Catastrophe*. New York: Times Books, 2004.

"Appropriators Call for Study on 'Asymmetric' Missile Threat." *Inside Missile Defense* 11, no. 26 (21 December 2005). http://web.lexis-nexis.com.

Barnard, Richard. "KEI Now Seen as Multipurpose Missile Defense Weapon." *Sea Power*, August 2004. http://www.navy league.org/sea_power/aug_04_09.php.

Barton, D. K. et al. *Report of the APS Study Group on Boost-Phase Intercept Systems for National Missile Defense: Scientific and Technical Issues*. American Physical Society, 5 October 2004. http://positron3.aps.org/media/press releases/upload/October-15-2004-BPI-Report.pdf.

Baucom, Donald. "The Rise and Fall of Brilliant Pebbles." *Journal of Social, Political, and Economic Studies* 29, no. 2 (Summer 2004): 145–90.

Boehlert (R-NY), Congressman Sherwood. *Opening Statement on NPOESS IG Report Hearing*. US House of Representatives, House Science and Technology Committee, Washington DC, 11 May 2006. http://gop.science.house.gov/hearings/full06/May%2011/sbopening.pdf.

"Boeing Receives Aircraft for Laser Gunship Program." *News Release*. The Boeing Company, 23 January 2006. http://www.boeing.com/ids/news/2006/q1/060123a_nr.html.

Burns, Robert. "Washington Talking to Warsaw about Defense." *Associated Press*, 16 November 2005. http://web.lexis-nexis.com/.

Burr, William, ed. *Missile Defense Thirty Years Ago: Déjà Vu All Over Again*, Washington, DC: National Security Archive, 18 December 2000. http://www.gwu.edu/~nsarchiv/NSAEBB/NSAEBB36/.

"Bush, India's Singh Sign Civil Nuclear Cooperation Agreement." *States News Service*, 2 March 2006. http://web.lexis-nexis.com/.

Butler, Amy. "Boosting Confidence." *Aviation Week and Space Technology* 163, no. 24 (19 December 2005). http://proquest.umi.com/.

Center for Defense Information. *Independent Review Team Findings and Recommendations, Presented to the Director, Missile Defense Agency*, 31 March 2005. http://www.cdi.org/pdfs/irt.pdf.

————. *Missile Defense Agency Fiscal Year 2007 (FY 07) Budget Estimate Overview*, February 2007. http://www.cdi.org/.

"China Says U.S. Weapons Sale to Taiwan Will Undermine Relations with Washington." *Associated Press Worldstream*, 28 September 2005. http://web.lexis-nexis.com/.

Cirincione, Joseph. "The Declining Ballistic Missile Threat, 2005." *Policy Outlook: Carnegie Non-Proliferation*, February 2005. http://www.carnegieendowment.org/files/DecliningBallisticMissileThreat2005-2.pdf.

Cohen, Stephen. *Failed Crusade: America and the Tragedy of Post-Communist Russia*. New York: W. W. Norton & Company, 2000.

Congressional Budget Office. *Alternatives for Boost Phase Missile Defense*. July 2004. http://www.cbo.gov/showdoc.cfm?index=5679&sequence=0.

Decker, Raymond J. *Defense Space Activities: Continuation of Evolved Expendable Launch Vehicle Program's Progress to Date Subject to Some Uncertainty*. United States General Accounting Office Report to Congressional Committees. GAO-04-778R. Washington, DC: General Accounting Office, 24 June 2004. http://www.gao.gov/new.items/d04778r.pdf.

Defense Acquisitions: Status of Ballistic Missile Defense Program in 2004. GAO-05-243. United States Government Accountability Office Report to Congressional Committees. Washington, DC: Government Accountability Office, March 2005. http://www.gao.gov/new.items/d05243.pdf.

Donovan, Michael. *Terrorism Project: Sadam's Scuds*. Center for Defense Information, 2 July 2002. http://www.cdi.org/terrorism/iraqmissile-pr.cfm.

Edwards, John, and Jack Kemp. *Russia's Wrong Direction: What the United States Can and Should Do.* Council on Foreign Relations, March 2006. http://www.cfr.org/publication/9997/.

Farah, Joseph. "Russia Equips Iran for War: Moscow Sells Tehran 29 Anti-missile Systems," *Worldnet Daily*, 2 December 2005. http://www.worldnetdaily.com/news/article.asp?ARTICLE_ID=47696.

Federation of American Scientists (FAS). "Address to the Nation on National Security by President Ronald Reagan, March 23, 1983." http://www.fas.org/spp/starwars/offdocs/rrspch.htm.

———. "China Nuclear Forces Guide, Nuclear: Nuclear Weapons," 29 November 2006. http://www.fas.org/nuke/guide/china/nuke/index.html.

———. *Executive Summary of the Report of the Commission to Assess the Ballistic Missile Threat to the United States.* Central Intelligence Agency, 15 July 1998. http://www.fas.org/irp/threat/bm-threat.htm.

———. *National Security Presidential Directive/NSPD-23: National Policy on Ballistic Missiles*, 16 December 2002. http://www.fas.org/irp/offdocs/nspd/nspd-23.htm.

———. *Report of the Panel on Reducing Risk in Ballistic Missile Defense Flight Test Programs*, 27 February 1998. http://www.fas.org/spp/starwars/program/welch/.

———. *Unclassified Summary of a National Intelligence Estimate: Foreign Missile Developments and the Ballistic Missile Threat through 2015.* National Intelligence Council, December 2001. http://www.fas.org/irp/nic/bmthreat-2015.htm.

Feickert, Andrew. *Missile Survey: Ballistic and Cruise Missiles of Foreign Countries.* Congressional Research Service, RL30427, 5 March 2004. http://fpc.state.gov/documents/organization/31999.pdf.

Flynn, Stephen E. "America the Vulnerable." *Foreign Affairs*, January/February 2002. http://www.foreignaffairs.org/20020101faessay6557/stephen-e-flynn/america-the-vulnerable.html.

Foster, Dr. John S., Jr., Mr. Earl Gjelde, Dr. William R. Graham, chairman, Dr. Robert J. Hermann, Mr. Henry (Hank) M. Kluepfel, Gen Richard L. Lawson, USAF (retired), Dr. Gordon

K. Soper, Dr. Lowell L. Wood Jr., and Dr. Joan B. Woodard. *Report to the House Armed Services Committee of the Commission to Assess the Threat to the United States from Electromagnetic Pulse (EMP) Attack.* Vol. 1, *Executive Report*, July 2004. http://www.iwar.org.uk/iwar/resources/emp/04-07 -22emp.pdf.

Garwin, Richard L. "Holes in the Missile Shield." *Scientific American* 291, no. 5 (November 2004). http://web.ebscohost.com/.

GlobalSecurity.org. "Weapons of Mass Destruction (WMD): A. Q. Khan." http://www.globalsecurity.org/wmd/world/ pakistan/khan.htm.

Goldgeier, James, and Michael McFaul. "What To Do About Russia." *Policy Review*, no. 133 (October/November 2005). http://web.ebscohost.com/.

Graham, Bradley. *Hit to Kill: The New Battle Over Shielding America from Missile Attack.* New York: Public Affairs, 2001.

Hali, S. M. "Should Pakistan Panic?" *The Nation* (Pakistan). Nawaiwaqt Group of News Papers, 29 March 2005. http:// www.nation.com.pk/daily/mar-2005/30/columns4.php.

Hildreth, Steven. *Kinetic Energy Kill for Ballistic Missile Defense: A Status Overview.* Congressional Research Service, RL33240, 18 January 2006. http://stinet.dtic.mil/cgi-bin/GetTRD oc?AD=ADA454467&Location=U2&doc=GetTRDoc.pdf.

Hodge, Nathan. "Sega Promises 'Back to Basics' in Ongoing Satellite Review." *Defense Daily*, 29 September 2005. http://proquest.umi.com/.

Hunt, Terrence. "Bush Celebrates India Nuclear Deal, Officials Say Next Stop in Pakistan Carries Risks." *Associated Press*, 2 March 2006. http://www.signonsandiego.com/news/ world/20060302-1637-bush.html.

Igarashi, Aya. "U.S. to Deploy Radar System Here within 6 Months." *Yomiuri Shimbun.* 8 February 2006. http://cnd yorks.gn.apc.org/yspace/articles/bmd/japan79.htm.

"Iran, China Study Political, Economic Cooperation." *BBC Monitoring*, 13 October 2005. http://web.lexis-nexis.com/.

"Iranian's 'Wipe Israel off Map' Words Prompt Sharp World Response." *Agence France-Presse*, 26 October 2005. http:// web.lexis-nexis.com/.

Ivanov, Sergei. "Russia Must Be Strong." *Wall Street Journal*, 11 January 2006. http://proquest.umi.com/.

Jamison, Phil. Office of the Secretary of Defense. Briefing. Subject: "US Policy on Missile Defense." National Defense Industrial Forum, 7 April 2005.

Kariya, Scott. "Patriot's Second Chance at Glory." *IEEE Spectrum* 5, vol. 4: (May 2003) 17–18.

Katz, Yaakov. "Arrow Can Now Intercept 'Any Iranian Missile'." *Jerusalem Post*, 3 March 2006. http://web.lexis-nexis .com/.

Katzman, Kenneth. *Iran: Arms and Weapons of Mass Destruction Suppliers*. Washington, DC: Congressional Research Service, 3 January 2003. http://www.fas.org/sgp/crs/ nuke/RL30551.pdf.

Krepon, Michael. *Cooperative Threat Reduction, Missile Defense, and the Nuclear Future*. New York: Palgrave Macmillan, 2003.

Kyl, Jon. "Unready for this Attack." *Washington Post*, 16 April 2005.

Langewiesche, William. "The Wrath of Khan: How AQ Kahn Made Pakistan a Nuclear Power—and Showed the Spread of Atomic Weapons Can't Be Stopped, Part I." *The Atlantic Monthly* 4, vol. 296 (November/December 2005) 62–85.

———. "The Wrath of Khan: How AQ Kahn Made Pakistan a Nuclear Power and Showed the Spread of Atomic Weapons Can't be Stopped, Part II." *Atlantic Monthly* 1, vol. 297 (January/February 2006) 96–118.

Levin, Robert E., director, Acquisition and Sourcing Management. "Space Acquisitions: Stronger Development Practices and Investment Planning Needed to Address Continuing Problems." GAO-05-891T. Testimony before the Strategic Forces Subcommittee, Committee on Armed Services, US House of Representatives. Washington, DC: US Government Accountability Office, 12 July 2005.

Liang, John. "Decision on Europe-based GMD Interceptor Site Could Come By April." *Inside Missile Defense*, 23 November 2005. http://web.lexis-nexis.com/.

Martin, Andrew. "Theater Ballistic Missiles and China's Doctrine of 'Active Defense'," *Jamestown Foundation, China Brief* 6, no. 6 (15 March 2006). http://www.jamestown .org/print_friendly.php?volume_id=415&issue_id=3654 &article_id=2370873.

Massachusetts Institute of Technology, Lincoln Laboratory. Seminar. "Ballistic Missile Defense Technology," 6–8 December 2005.

"MDA Director Outlines Allocation of Fiscal Year 2006 Budget Increases." *Inside the Pentagon* 22, no. 7 (16 February 2006). http://web.lexis-nexis.com/.

"Megatons to Megawatts Eliminates Equivalent of 10,000 Nuclear Warheads; President Bush Cites Program as Model of U.S.-Russian Cooperation; America's Utilities Operating Nuclear Power Plants Make the Program Successful." *Business Wire, Inc.*, 21 September 2005. http://www.encyclopedia.com/doc/1G1-136465535.html.

Meyer, Henry. "Russian Defense Minister Confirms Missile Sale to Iran." *Associated Press*, 5 December 2005.

Miller, John J. "Israel's Arrow Defense: How Israel Has Prepared for the Next Strike." *National Review Online*, 15 October 2002. http://www.nationalreview.com/miller/miller101502.asp.

Miller, Steven, and Dmitri Trenin, eds. *The Russian Military: Power and Policy*. Cambridge, MA: MIT Press, 2004.

Missile Defense Agency. "History of Ballistic Missile Defense." http://www.mda.mil/mdalink/html/history.html.

MissileThreat.com. "Statement of the Honorable Henry A. Kissinger before the Senate Foreign Relations Committee, 26 May 1999." http://www.missilethreat.com/resources/pageID.262/default.asp.

Morgan, Benjamin. "China's Economy Likely One of World's Top Five after Strong 2005." *Agence France-Presse*, 23 January 2006. http://web.lexis-nexis.com/.

Nuclear Threat Institute. *WMD411: Your Information Resource on Nuclear, Biological and Chemical Weapons Issues, Policy Options—Iran*. Washington, DC: Monterey Institute, Center for Nonproliferation Studies, 28 July 2003. http://www.nti.org/f_wmd411/f2e1.html.

"Obering: Decision Forthcoming to Give MDA Cruise Missile Defense." *Inside Missile Defense* 11, no. 26 (21 December 2005). http://web.lexis-nexis.com/.

Obering, Lt Gen Henry A., III, USAF, director, Missile Defense Agency. "Ballistic Missile Defense of the US Homeland." Address. 35th Institute for Foreign Policy Analysis/The Fetcher

School, Tufts University, Conference on National Security Strategy and Policy: Planning for and Responding to Threats to the US Homeland, Washington, DC, 28–29 October 2004. http://www.fletcherconference.com/oldtranscripts/2004/obering.htm. http://www.fletcherconference.com/old powrpoint/2004/Obering28Oct.ppt.

Office of the Secretary of Defense. *Annual Report to Congress: The Military Power of the People's Republic of China, 2005.* Washington, DC: Government Printing Office, 2005. http://www.defenselink.mil/news/Jul2005/d20050719china.pdf.

Office of the Under Secretary of Defense for Acquisition, Technology, and Logistics. *Report of the Defense Science Board Task Force on Patriot System Performance: Report Summary,* January 2005. http://www.acq.osd.mil/dsb/reports/2005-01-Patriot_Report_Summary.pdf.

Onishi, Norimitsu. "US Confirms Test of Missiles Was Conducted By North Korea." *New York Times,* 9 March 2006.

"Opening Statement By John Conyers Jr., Committee On Government Operations Subcommittee On Legislation And National Security An Oversight Hearing On The Performance Of The Patriot Missile In The Gulf War." US House of Representatives, Washington, DC: 7 April 1992. http://www.fas.org/spp/starwars/congress/1992_h/h920407c.htm.

Oster, Shai. "China Plans 15% Boost in Military Spending." *Wall Street Journal,* 6 March 2006.

Pasztor, Andy. "U.S.'s Lofty Plans for Smart Satellites Fall Back to Earth." *Wall Street Journal,* 11 February 2006.

"Perspectives on Complex-System Engineering." *Collaborations: Inside Knowledge for MITRE's System Engineering Community* 3, no. 2 (June 2005). http://www.necsi.org/necsi/mitrecoll3.2.pdf.

Roosevelt, Ann. "MDA Moves Forward on Research Efforts with Japan." *Defense Daily.* 23 December 2005. http://www.accessmylibrary.com/coms2/summary_0286-12407001_ITM.

———. "MDA Requests $10.4 Billion in FY '07 for Its Part in the 'Long War'." *Defense Daily,* 9 February 2006. http://www.missiledefenseadvocacy.org/index/news/current/MDA2007Budget.html.

Rumsfeld, Donald, secretary of Defense. *Quadrennial Defense Review Report.* Washington, DC: Department of Defense, 6 February 2006. http://www.comw.org/qdr/qdr2006.pdf.

Schneider, Mark. *The Nuclear Forces and Doctrine of the Russian Federation.* Publication no. 003. US Nuclear Strategy Forum, Washington, DC: National Institute Press, January 2006. http://www.nipp.org/Adobe/Russian%20nuclear%20doctrine%20-%20NSF%20for%20print.pdf.

Sieff, Mark. "BMD Focus: Russia Rattles Missile Treaty." *United Press International,* 2 March 2006. http://cndyorks.gn.apc.org/yspace/articles/bmd/russia_rattles_missile_treaty.htm.

———. "BMD Watch: Nuke SCUD threat to U.S." *United Press International,* 8 November 2005. http://www.spacewar.com/news/abm-05zm.html.

Smith, Marcia. *Military Space Programs: Issues Concerning DoD's SBIRS and STSS Programs.* Congressional Research Service, RS21148, 25 November 2005. http://www.cnie.org/NLE/CRSreports/06feb/RS21148.pdf.

Tirpak, John A. "The Airborne Laser Narrows Its Beam." *Air Force Magazine* 89, no.12 (December 2006). http://www.afa.org/magazine/dec2006/1206laser.pdf.

Trachtenberg, David. "Off the Radar: Missile Defense Was the Administration's 'Highest Priority.' What Happened?" *Armed Forces Journal,* January 2006. http://www.armedforcesjournal.com/2006/01/1408410/.

"Troubled Airborne Laser Program on Track for 2008 Missile Test." *Inside Missile Defense* 12, no. 5 (1 March 2006). http://www.militaryphotos.net/forums/showthread.php?t=74321.

Union of Concerned Scientists, *Missile Defense,* 7 September 2005. http://www.ucsusa.org/global_security/missile_defense.

US House. *Republican Contract with America.* Republican Members of the House of Representatives, 1994. http://www.house.gov/house/Contract/CONTRACT.html.

Wirtz, James, and Jeffrey Larsen, eds. *Rockets' Red Glare: Missile Defense and the Future of World Politics.* Cambridge, MA: Westview Press, 2001.

The White House. "National Policy on Ballistic Missile Defense Fact Sheet." 20 May 2003. http://www.whitehouse.gov/news/releases/2003/05/20030520-15.html.

Yanarella, Ernest J. *The Missile Defense Controversy: Strategy, Technology, and Politics, 1955–1972.* Lexington, KY: The University Press of Kentucky, 1977.

The Influence of Politics, Technology, and Asia on the Future of US Missile Defense

Air University Press Team

Chief Editor
Jim Howard

Copy Editor
Lula Barnes

Cover Art and Book Design
Steven C. Garst

Illustrations
Daniel Armstrong

*Composition and
Prepress Production*
Ann Bailey

Quality Review
Tammi Long

Print Preparation
Joan Hickey

Distribution
Diane Clark

www.ingramcontent.com/pod-product-compliance
Lightning Source LLC
Chambersburg PA
CBHW080106010626
45794CB00015B/3136